SHOULD I GET MY BABY BAPTIZED?

A CHRISTIAN PARENTING GUIDE
BY BEN KNISKERN

DEDICATED TO:

DEPUTY SHERIFF KURT B. WYMAN
1987 - 2011
KILLED IN THE LINE OF DUTY: JUNE 7, 2011

CONTENTS

Chapter

Chapter One

TO CHRISTEN
OR NOT TO CHRISTEN

The question of the necessity of baptizing infants has been an ongoing debate since 200 AD. That's over 1,800 years, and really, the battle is still going strong. There is no end in sight either, because all of the information we now have on the subject is probably all the information we will have until the end of time. Fortunately, people aren't brutally killing each other over baptisms any longer — at least not in America anyway.

There was a time in history when "religious" groups would actually persecute and kill people who, even though they had been baptized or christened as an infant, decided they wanted to be re-baptized as an adult. They were called Anabaptists, which simply means "one who wants to be baptized over again." These ones who felt the need to be re-baptized had come to a personal faith in Jesus Christ as adults and believed their infant baptism didn't mean anything. Now that they understood what it meant to be a Christian, they decided to have a true believer's baptism.

The main reason for the conflict back then — as well as today — is that there isn't any written order from God that says either, "You must get your baby baptized," or "You should not get your baby baptized." So, we are left to make up our own minds on the subject based on the information we have. It appears that there are a number of clues that can help us make the right decision, but the clues do not involve what *people* say about it so much as they do what *God* says about it. Unfortunately, most people don't do any personal research to discover the facts, but simply proceed based on what they are taught, tradition, or personal beliefs.

As far as beliefs, you'd have to wonder why else anyone would consider infant baptism if not for the belief that this might — or must be — a requirement for a child to go to Heaven someday. It sounds a little like fire insurance, or even more like prepaying college tuition. Pay for it now so it's all taken care of when the time comes.

That's an interesting concept, and even better if it works. My family has always been big on infant baptism. My ancestors were German Lutheran immigrants who arrived in America in 1710. We have great family history records because they baptized every child that was born here in America for almost the next 200 years. It was automatic for them.

The biggest question is, I guess, what good did it do? First of all, almost anyone who gets their baby baptized will fall under one of two main categories. The first category is those who believe there is a God and that the Bible is a valid source of His desires. Those in this group have good intentions. They may either feel they are protecting their child's soul from hell, or believe that by having them christened they will always be Christians. This can create, among other things, a false sense of security. No one can guarantee what a child will grow up to become. I doubt very much when Adolph Hitler's parents had him christened that they ever dreamed their bouncing baby boy would one day be responsible for the deaths of more than 12 million people — 25 percent of which were children. It seems clear that if our goal is to have them be Christians, then there has to be more to it than infant baptism. It certainly didn't work for Mr. and Mrs. Hitler. It might be that the only hope for our children to reach this goal will be by our intervention as parents, revealing God to them as they are raised.

The second group contains those who baptize their baby for reasons such as that's the way their religion does things; uncertainty; fear; or because they are urged on (even bullied) by their parents, family, or friends. Those who are heavy into religion would not even question the necessity of such a practice. They are taught that this is what you should do and they just do it. Those who are uncertain about spiritual things can feel that they might not be giving their baby the protection they need and act on the fear of the potential eternal consequences.

The people that consider this question or face their fears and try to figure out what the real truth is — rather than just doing it because that's what other people do — are wise. This book is designed to help those who truly care about the eternal future of their children and want to do everything they possibly can to help them make their way successfully through this life and into the next, which will be with Jesus in Heaven. That's the goal. Not just my goal for this book, but the goal for every parent who is truly concerned about the spiritual welfare of their children as well.

I am honored that you are trusting me to show you the right way. Some may ask, "Why should I trust you?" That's a good question, too. In my defense, I have been studying this subject for eighteen years. If I studied another subject that long, you might trust me to transplant a lung or even council your marriage. I take this subject very seriously because I have a heart for souls in general, but I am especially concerned about the spiritual welfare of young people. In fact, I have been working with young people and their spiritual development for eighteen years as well. In that time I have never met one teenager that has benefited even slightly from being baptized as a baby.

So what do we do then? Just forget it? Absolutely not. There is much you can do for your baby in place of a ritualistic baptism that holds no spiritual value — in reality, very much. There are steps that you can take now so that when your child grows up, he or she will not be a spiritually lost teenager like most — if not all — of the ones who were baptized as infants. Teenagers that grow up running from God will also run from their parents, and as they phase into young adulthood, they will run toward all the wrong kinds of things. Things that you — as you hold your baby and glance into their sweet little eyes — could never have imagined would be possible.

One of the things that concern me most is that once a child has been raised and heads out on their own, they should at that point be able to hit the ground running toward an abundant, fulfilling, successful life. Instead, however, the majority of young people today that leave home spend years rehabilitating from the physical and emotional scarring brought on by their dysfunctional childhood, and most never do completely recover. As a parent, your job for the next twenty-one years or so will be to lead your child toward adulthood undamaged by the world. It would be far better for your child to enter adult life not having to recover from the scars of an improper upbringing.

> ...parents who have wise children are glad because of them.
>
> ~Proverbs 23:24

That's why it is so vitally important that instead of baptizing them for Christ now, which is pointless, you spend that energy preparing them for Christ in the future. You would be surprised how much spiritual good you can do for your baby right now. You've probably heard that if you read to your baby while they are still in the womb it can be helpful to their mental development. Why would anybody believe *that*, and not believe that you can start teaching them about God while they are still very young? A child that grows up knowing that God is real typically won't run from God, and a child that is not running from God will typically not run from their parents either. Instead, they will be friends with their parents and give their parents joy. As I work with young people, I find very few that are giving their parents any joy, but see very many running from them and even at war with them.

Is there something that we can do to interrupt this cycle? I know we can't really do much to help other families that are having problems with *their* children, but is there a way that we can take steps now to help make it possible that, down the road, our family might have peace among *its* members? I must caution you that there probably is no perfect family. However, even though I know families that have or have had children in juvenile detention facilities, I also know families that have their children spending their summers working at Christian camps helping others. I know teenagers that have pledged sexual purity until marriage, as well as girls as young as thirteen years old that have become pregnant. I personally know teenagers that stand on corners and hand out Bible tracts and tell people about Jesus, while I also know teenagers that stand on corners and sell drugs. As you hold your baby in your arms and contemplate the future, which scenario in these comparisons sounds better to you? You may not be able to build a perfect family, but with God's help you can build a much better one than if you leave it up to chance.

The worst-sounding sides of these couplets are what will most likely happen — just by default. This is what children by and large run to when they are left to raise themselves. The odds are stacked against having happy kids interacting in a loving family where there is no word from God. Now I know that it is possible to raise a good kid that is buried in their schoolwork, sports, and activities without including God in the equation, but there is also a Bible verse that asks what profit it is for an individual to gain the whole world and lose their own soul. What good is it? I often hear people say what a good job so and so did with their children. And it is true. They're not in jail; they're not hooked on drugs; they're polite; they may not even have any body art or piercings.

But what about their spiritual position in life? A good person who was raised well and dies without Christ will suffer the same fate as a felon in Sing Sing who dies without Christ. That's not my rule; that's God's rule. I learned a long time ago that there is no point in trying to argue with God over His rules. The best bet is to learn them and keep them. He is not going to budge on any of them when it is time for judgment. When that day comes, the guilty will stand before Him for sentencing, not trial. There won't be any debating about whether a person was good or not. A guilty verdict is handed down at death to everyone who dies without knowing Christ, no matter how good of a life or how bad of a life they lived. Their eternal fate is sealed at that point.

By the same token, anyone who dies that has a believer's relationship with Christ will immediately go to be with Him and enjoy being a joint heir of God with Christ forever. Your child's best chance to avoid the unbeliever's fate is to learn from *you* how to become one of these heirs of God. At this moment you may not feel all that qualified to teach them about these spiritual matters. Because of that, I have compiled quite a few good ideas that will help you become an expert in raising your child in the teaching of the Lord. First, though, just in case you have any question whatsoever left in your mind about infant baptism, we will take a really close look at that subject and clear this up first before we move on.

Chapter Two

VARIOUS REASONS

When you're thinking about getting your baby baptized, you have to ask yourself, "What good will it do?" What is the end result that you are hoping for? I searched around a little to find out what parents give as reasons for getting a baby baptized. Here are some that I found:

1. Just in case
2. Marking the baby as belonging to Christ - Baptizing them now will make it so they will always be a Christian
3. To protect their soul - It saves them from hell
4. It's what my religion expects - It's required
5. It's what my parents, family, or friends expect
6. It guarantees my baby a place in Heaven
7. It cleanses a baby from original sin
8. The Bible says to - Christ has commanded it
9. I (the parent) was baptized as a baby
10. It will help them later on if they stray from God - It will help lead them back to Christ

There may be more reasons than this — I'm sure — but these seem to be the ones most widely expressed.

Let's take a brief look at each of these reasons to see how much credence they might hold.

1. JUST IN CASE

I guess the first thing you have to ask is, "Just in case what?" Just in case they die? Just in case there really is a God? Just in case God really expects it, or just in case it may help something? If just in case is the only reason someone can come up with to baptize a baby, then they might as well skip it altogether. This is like saying, "I will pray, just in case there is a God that will hear," or "I will believe in God, just in case there is a Heaven or Hell." If you're baptizing your baby when you truly don't believe there is a benefit, then this has got to be the worst reason of all. If nothing else, you (and your child later in life) will feel there's no need for further spiritual contact with God since they've already taken care of the "just in case" part. That's the way my parents felt. I was baptized as a baby, so I was all set. Case closed. Those that believe this way neglect to feel the need for checking out the Bible to see if there might be a little something else that God might expect from them.

2. MARKING THE BABY AS BELONGING TO CHRIST - BAPTIZING THEM NOW SO THEY WILL ALWAYS BE A CHRISTIAN

This is a two-part, same thought type reason. First, all babies automatically belong to Christ, whether they are baptized or not. They don't need to be marked in order for God to recognize them or be set apart for Him by human ritual. God alone does the setting apart for Himself. God told Jeremiah that before he was even placed in his mother's womb that He—God—knew him, and had set him apart for His service. This was not just before he was born, but before he was formed.

Years prior to that, after King David's infant son died, he said, "Someday I will go to him, but he cannot come back to me" (2 Samuel 12:23). We can safely reason that David, "a man after God's own heart," would someday be going to Heaven. David's baby would be there waiting, having gone on ahead of him, even though never having been baptized. These are more than just isolated incidents; they are examples for us. The New Testament teaches that everything that was written in the Old Testament was written for out instruction.

Second, baptizing them now so that they'll always be a Christian is not a valid reason at all. Today, the meaning of the word Christian has a slightly looser definition than it did in the late first century when the New Testament was written. Believers in Christ were first called Christians (followers of Christ) at a place called Antioch, which was located in what is today known as southern Turkey. These people were given this name because they acted like devoted followers—or imitators—of Christ. In order to be true followers of Christ (Christians), they had to learn and follow His teachings with conviction. This obviously is not possible for an infant in any case. A baby's only hope of becoming a Christian is to learn about Christ and, consequently, believe in Him. Whether they are baptized or not, in order to become a Biblical Christian, they must decide in their heart that Jesus died on the cross for their sin and that God raised Him from the dead. No matter what any religion or instructor teaches you, this is the only way a baby will someday become a Christian.

3. TO PROTECT THEIR SOUL - IT SAVES
THEM FROM HELL

As we mentioned earlier, every baby's soul is pro-
tected by God. As far as we know from anything that
God has revealed to us, that protection remains with a
baby until they reach the age where they clearly understand the difference between right and wrong. We call it
"the age of accountability." Whatever age that is—and
we suspect that it is different for each individual child—
this is when it becomes vitally important that a child
has already become a Christian. If they reach this age
and die without Christ, then we have failed big-time as
parents. It is our job to make sure that by the time they
reach this age, they are begging to have Christ as their
Savior and understand completely that there really is a
Hell, and it is *not* the place they want to end up in.

Imagine one person standing before God (which
the Bible says that we all must do someday) and trying
to explain that they were baptized as a baby so all the
wrong things that they have done throughout their
whole life should not be counted against them. Imagine
a second person standing beside the first person who
did all the same sinful things, but this second one never
got baptized as an infant. Could anybody really think
that God would condemn that second person to Hell
and let the first person enter Heaven?

If the Bible taught that, then that's what we would
have to believe. But that is not what the Bible teaches at
all. This is in fact a salvation by "works" heresy that has
plagued the Christian church since the first century AD.
It is so much easier to teach that we can do something
to save ourselves or others (in this case, our babies) then
it is to teach that we can have salvation only through
our faith in Christ—that it is God's gift of grace to all

who believe in Him. I imagine at least part of the reason this whole idea of infant baptism came into being was to lessen parental responsibility. Otherwise, churches would have to teach that the best chance a child has of becoming a Christian is if the child's parents pour their whole life into them. That would mean in order to do it right, you would have to give up on all your own plans until you are done raising your child, because raising a child for Christ is a fulltime job. It is much easier to teach that you can simply baptize them and then get on with your own life.

It is noble to want to protect your child from Hell. It is far nobler to be willing to spend whatever time it takes to accomplish that mission.

4. IT'S WHAT MY RELIGION EXPECTS - IT'S REQUIRED

They say it's required, but really, what is it required for? Unfortunately, we are now getting closer to the heart of the matter. Many religions teach that infant baptism is mandatory — mandatory for many of the reasons that we have been discussing, as well as, in many cases, mandatory for joining their particular denomination.

There are several reasons that a church denomination would demand this obedience. One, of course, might be that they really believe they are doing the right thing. I'm sure that in many cases church leaders are innocent of any intentional misleading.

On the other hand, many churches are run like a business. With that in mind, there may be as many as 13 million babies baptized each year. It's hard to tell for sure, but based on the estimated number of baptisms that each denomination reports, it seems like a reasonable guess.

It doesn't seem like baptizing should be a money thing. If someone is going to be baptized into the family of God, you would think there shouldn't be a price tag placed on that God-given privilege. Contrary to that, however, it can cost between 50 and 100 dollars to get your baby baptized today. That represents a minimum of 650 million dollars in revenues for churches each year. For those churches that seem to be in existence to make money, it is no wonder that they promote this ritual as being required. It may be coincidence only, but most churches that require infant baptism also place a high emphasis on income.

In the Bible, where baptism is first introduced, there are no fees mentioned. You might think, *Well, things cost more today and churches need more money,* but the fact is that people in the first century church could have used any money they could get their hands on. While the religious leaders of the day were selling animals at an inflated rate for sacrifice and the money changers were charging a high transfer rate to change foreign money into currency accepted by the temple authorities, the believers in Christ were baptizing people for free. They were baptizing people with joy because they were having a part in growing the kingdom of Christ, not because they were interested in padding their robes with a little extra cash.

Whether it's a genuine desire to see souls added to Heaven or an easy way to make some quick cash, denominations that require infant baptism and expect to be paid for it are not following the true teaching of the Bible and should be avoided. Nowhere in the Bible is it stated that we are required to baptize our young children. This is a teaching that has been introduced to society by man, not God. It was this kind of teaching that led to the final destruction of Jerusalem in 70 AD.

The religious leaders of that day taught their own doc-trines—the teachings of men—rather than the teach-ings of God. They expected people to follow *their* rules, rather than God's rules. It's much the same with many religions today, and not just on the subject of infant baptism.

5. IT'S WHAT MY PARENTS, FAMILY, OR FRIENDS EXPECT

Chances are somebody on one family side or the other is going to want you to have your baby bap-tized or christened. The law of averages is against you. Family members and friends can be persuasive or even downright pushy at times, but this is your baby and you cannot let others make this decision for you. After you have learned all you can about this subject, you will be able to make an educated decision based on your knowledge of the subject combined with considering the advice of others. It is true that you should always honor your parents, but—in cases like this—it may be better to listen to your parent's advice (honoring them) and then weigh that advice against what the Bible says. Somebody at some point is not going to be happy, but doing what is biblically correct and pleasing God far outweighs any other decision you could make.

6. IT GUARANTEES MY BABY A PLACE IN HEAVEN

Based on what we have learned so far, all babies already have a place in Heaven, so baptizing them for this reason would not make any sense. As far as a future place in Heaven, once your baby is old enough to be accountable for their own sin, gaining entrance to Heaven is a little more detailed than just being baptized. Jesus told His followers that when He left here, He was going to prepare a place for them (and us) in Heaven. Because of this, we know for sure that not only is there is a place called Heaven, but also that Jesus has prepared a place there for all who believe in Him. He also said that He is the doorway to Heaven. In order to reach there, we have to pass through Him. He told his follower, Thomas, "...I am the way, and the truth, and the life. The only way to the Father is through me" (John 14:6). Of course, God the Father is in Heaven. We will discuss this a little further in the coming chapters, but it is important to understand that there is an exact standard for entrance into Heaven. There is no guess work, such as hopefully you had your baby baptized in the right religion; hopefully it was the right church; hopefully it was done in the right way. All of those reasons are subject to human interpretation and have nothing to do with what is required for entrance into God's Heaven. Man's heaven maybe, but man's heaven is only a made-up place designed to match what a human mind can come up with. You can tell the difference easily, because man's heaven has different rules for entrance depending on whom you listen to or who you ask. God's Heaven only has one unchanging rule that is specifically spelled out in the Bible so that there can be no mistake. This is a thread that we will unravel together as we go through the following chapters.

7. IT CLEANSES A BABY FROM ORIGINAL SIN

The Bible has a pretty clear teaching on sin. Actually, the entire Bible deals with this subject. At least one reason is that it is sin that separates man from God. God is holy. He is without sin. Man, on the other hand, is sinful. Dunking a baby in water—or anyone for that matter—is not going to take care of a problem that the entire Bible is written about. God could have taken care of that with one sheet of paper. Actually one sentence. "Get your baby baptized and that will take care of it." That could be Genesis 1:1 and the first and only verse in the Bible. But it doesn't say that. God goes to great lengths to explain the situation of sin, from its entrance into the world to what ultimately needs to be done about it. While we are here on planet earth, there are only two things that the Bible teaches that can cleanse us from sin.

The blood of Christ that was shed for us on the cross at Calvary is the first. This is the blood sacrifice that is required by God to set you free from your sin. When you come to an understanding that what Jesus did on the cross was all that is needed to set you free from sin and death, you are no longer responsible for the payment which is due for your sin. Jesus paid that for you. Unfortunately, though—and this is the second thing—you still reside in your flesh body which inherited sin from your parents at its conception. Because of this, even though you have God-empowered self-control through His spirit that now resides with your spirit, you will still make mistakes and sin. 1 John 1:9 says, "But if we confess our sins, he will forgive our sins, because we can trust God to do what is right. He will cleanse us from all the wrongs we have done."

An infant cannot understand what Jesus did on the cross at Calvary for them, nor can they understand the concept of confession for forgiveness. So, until they are old enough to understand their need to have Jesus as their Savior and understand that they have to confess any sins they are aware of once they do have Jesus as their Savior, cleansing from sin is not possible. It is also not necessary until they are old enough to know about and comprehend these things. At the point that they are old enough to get it, though, you need to make sure that you have done everything in your power to prepare them to make this decision for Christ. If they get there and are not prepared, they will likely reject the whole idea and move on. After that, it's not pretty. Carry your baby into a juvenile detention facility and think about where this baby could be in seventeen years or so without proper direction. Don't count on schools, programs, sports, or even churches to lead your child to a God-centered life of peace and love. Parents of the 71 thousand children in juvenile detention centers in the United States today were counting on these very same things to lead their children in the right direction. Chances are that very few of these children were raised from infancy to understand their need to have a personal relationship with Jesus Christ. It is likely that their parents did not understand this critical life ingredient either. In so doing, they have left the Heaven-bound future of their children to chance, and in serious doubt.

8. THE BIBLE SAYS TO - CHRIST HAS COMMANDED IT

This is simply not true. Whoever is telling you this either does not read the Bible themselves and only assumes it to be true, or they are purposely lying to you. The Bible teaches two things about baptism, and both of these relate to believing in Jesus.

The first thing is that after you come to truly understand the Gospel (the Good News of Jesus Christ) — that He died in your place as a sacrifice for your sin, was buried, and three days later that He rose from the dead, then you should be baptized by being submerged in water. As Jesus was preparing to go back to Heaven, He told His followers. "Go everywhere in the world, and tell the Good News to everyone. Anyone who believes and is baptized will be saved, but anyone who does not believe will be punished" (Mark 16:15-16). This is the only command about baptism from Jesus. It's not for babies. He said to tell the Good News (His death, burial and resurrection), and anyone who believes and is baptized will be saved.

There is a longstanding debate on whether you should be immersed in, poured over, or sprinkled with water. That debate has been going on as long as the debate over whether or not it's right to baptize babies. I always say that things walk hand in hand. Groups that have right teaching generally have *all* right teaching. Groups that have one wrong teaching generally have more than one wrong teaching. That's just the way it seems to go. It stands to reason that all of the groups that believe in infant baptism also believe in sprinkling or pouring water on those being baptized. By the same token, the groups that understand the Biblical truth about baptism are the same ones that believe that the original meaning of our word *baptism* was to dip or immerse in water.

Since being baptized is an outward display of your inward faith and trust in Jesus and what He did for you on the cross at Calvary, and an act of obedience to Jesus, the actual process itself will not hamper your salvation. It will, however, hamper your involvement with groups that require baptism by immersion in order to join their fellowship. The reason they have this rule is that in order to be baptized by immersion, you first have to profess your faith in Jesus Christ as your Lord and Savior. By wanting to be baptized, you are declaring that you understand that Jesus died for you, was buried, and rose from the dead. You are in turn dying to self, burying your old sinful life, and rising to a new life in Christ. It's hard to give that picture of your faith as you're getting sprinkled, and confessing Jesus as your Savior is not normally required for this procedure. So, you can see why Bible-believing churches would want to have baptism by immersion as part of their membership qualifications. It's a lot easier to raid the sheep pen when the door's not guarded.

It's not foolproof. Plenty of evil and false teaching does sneak into a Bible-believing church, even when they require baptism by immersion and a confession of faith in Jesus in order to join their fellowship. People still lie and get baptized by immersion, but God knows the heart and He knows the ones who genuinely trust in Him. All liars that have ever lived and died have now been dealt with for the harm they've done.

9. I (THE PARENT) WAS BAPTIZED AS A BABY

Oftentimes, because a parent was christened, they feel their babies should be christened as well. That may sound logical on the surface, but as you think about it, what actual good has it done for them? They want their baby christened so that they will belong to Christ and have a spot in Heaven, but do they themselves belong to Christ? Are they even sure that they will go to Heaven someday? It is possible that their parents were hoping the exact same thing for them that they are hoping for their child now. If christening didn't help them find their way to God, how will it help their child? Don't let yourself get caught in this quagmire. This is a vicious family circle that will continue until somebody breaks the chain. Obviously, since many people do belong to Christ and are sure that they will go to

Heaven someday, there must be a way—other than christening, which does not work—to achieve this goal.

10. IT WILL HELP THEM LATER ON IF THEY STRAY FROM GOD - IT WILL HELP LEAD THEM BACK TO CHRIST

First of all, I think we've pretty much discovered that it is not *if* they stray from God at all. We are all born straying from God. I, myself, was a fairly devious child. Many of my friends were as well. We were all baptized as infants, but as we grew up, we ran from God. I was reminded often that I was baptized as a baby and my name was on the church's "cradle role." The thing is, once I got to the age where I understood right from wrong and knew that there were consequences for my sin, I was responsible for them. If I died then, I would be dying with never having asked Jesus Christ to be my Savior and—baptism or no baptism—at that point I would have been looking at eternity in Hell. This is true of any infant that is baptized and then grows up running from God. The baptism that an infant has is powerless to save them from Hell. Only faith in Christ can do that, and I know I didn't get that with my infant baptism or cradle role placement.

Can infant baptism possibly lead a child back to Christ though? It's very unlikely. Children that are baptized as infants are often left to develop spiritually on their own. Denominations that follow up baptism with other rituals are most times devoid spiritually. They may have many steps, exercises, performances, or procedures that you can do to build yourself up to a high religious level, but they are essentially bereft of any true spiritual meaning. Kids are not stupid and so usually they come to an understanding quite early that all this religious mumbo jumbo is not going to do anything for them and it has no real value. Really, they could care less. If they are doing anything that looks right, they are merely going through the motions in order to get it over with. They end up spiritually bankrupt because they have spent all of their youth trying to gain something that just isn't there.

I imagine when we're trying to decide whether or not baby baptism is the right thing to do, we're not considering that aspect so much. All of us, when we have children, are pretty much brand new at it. We have no experience with raising children, and if we're going to be truthful about it, if we have to ask the question, "Should I get my baby baptized?" we probably don't have all that much experience spiritually either. So here we are. Spiritually challenged ourselves and making a monumental spiritual decision for the future of our baby without any true understanding of the implications.

I'm not condemning anybody here; I did the same thing. A short while after my daughter was born, I started thinking seriously about the need to have her christened. I have to admit also that I don't really know why. I guess I was either thinking that this was what the Lord would want me to do, or that by doing this, God would look more favorably down upon her. Fortunately, God led me in a different direction and literally saved me from myself, and in so doing saved my child from myself at the same time. The way things have turned out could have been drastically different if I had gone through with the christening and left my daughter's spiritual growth to chance.

We can safely conclude that people straying from God do not find their way back to Him because they were christened when they were babies. I encourage you to ask people you know that are living for Jesus now how they found their way to God. Not one will mention christening. Actually, in many cases, the opposite is true.

Chapter Three

NOWHERE TO RUN - NOWHERE TO HIDE

*B*elieve it or not, there is a worldwide movement happening now for adults who were christened as babies to have themselves officially de-baptized. Adults can either go to a de-baptizing priest to have a cere-mony performed with a hairdryer that blows the waters of baptism away, or they can simply go to a website, fill out some information, and download a printable, official certificate of de-baptism. Although this sounds crazy, it is happening. Christening has not led these adults who are now atheists back to God as intended, but further away. I'm not sure how far a person needs to stoop in order to bring themselves to a point where they are willing to mock God, but whether christening an infant is right or wrong, de-baptizing is not an intel-ligent thing to take part in.

The Bible says that the fear of the Lord is the begin-ning of wisdom (Proverbs 9:10). Arrogantly thumbing your nose at God is not showing a great deal of fear or wisdom. When you consider that someday every knee will bow before God and confess that Jesus Christ is Lord (Romans 14:11), imagine the egg on the faces of those involved with de-baptizing when that day arrives. If they don't really believe in God, then it doesn't seem like it would matter to them whether they had been baptized as an infant or not. It is more likely that they do believe in God but would prefer to have nothing to do with Him. It must be that by being de-baptized, they feel they are ridding themselves of God's presence in their lives. Unfortunately for them, there's just nowhere to run from God's presence. All they are doing in my estimation is begging for trouble, and when the trouble comes, there won't be anywhere to hide from it either.

There are many events in human history that teach about the dangers of taking a blatant stand against God. It's hard to say what the most notable was, but some of the more memorable ones are when Eve sided with Satan and ate the forbidden fruit (the outcome was the fall of man and the introduction of sin into the world); the whole world rebelled against God during the time of Noah (the result was that the earth was flooded and everyone perished except Noah, seven family members, and representatives of all other living species); the tower of Babel, where most of the world once again staged a rebellion against God (the result was that God confused the language and scattered the people around the world); Korah, who lead a revolt against Moses and Aaron, God's chosen leaders, which lead to the ground opening up and swallowing Korah and his followers alive down into the pit (supposed by many to be Hell); and Beltashazzer, King of Babylon, who challenged God by drinking from the gold cups that were stolen from God's temple, (the result of which led to his death and the loss of the Babylonian Kingdom to the Meads and Persians).

And so, just like we might ask, "What is the point of christening a baby?" we might also ask, "What is the

34

point of getting de-baptized?" Without really under-standing the subject, it's tough to know what to do. We certainly don't want to put our child in a position where they might want to get de-baptized someday. In a few years, that movement may grow to monstrous proportions, and "everybody" may be doing it because it's the cool thing to do. We're told if we don't get our child christened, they will have no association with God, and now we find that if we do, it may push them even further away from God than if they had not been christened in the first place. What can we do for our child who is now right in the middle of this spiritual battle for their soul?

If you're like I was, then you pretty much have no clue. You have a child that you want to grow up to be a Christian and eventually spend eternity in Heaven. Although you're not even sure yet what the first step is, you have been given the awesome responsibility of leading this child to Christ. That's now your job. It's your lot in life if you choose to accept it. It's the mis-sion God has sent you on, and it's going to be tough. Especially since—unless you've already raised one family and are starting a second—you've never done this before.

Although difficult, it's not nearly as difficult as it may seem right now, especially if your child is still an infant. If you have children that are older, the level of difficulty becomes that much greater. The reason is, as children grow, they develop their own mindset based on their surroundings. But whether your children are very young, or older, you still need to face this respon-sibility and give it your all. If you trust in God, He will help you learn to do what you must do in order to raise your children the way He expects you to. No matter who you are, when God gives you a mission, He will always give you the abilities you need — as well as stay right by your side — to see it all the way through. That is a promise from God's Word.

When you get to the end of the road, if you go out with time to reflect, what is going to matter to you? From hearing the testimonies of others, I know it is not going to be how much money you made, how far you advanced in your career, or how big your house was. Even the bulk of your accomplishments are not going to mean anything at that point. Your biggest concern at the end of your life is going to be how you raised your children. You'll wonder, "Did I do all I could to point them toward God? Are they living for God and serving Him with their lives? Do they know Jesus as Savior? Is there anything I could have done differently?"

That's about all that is going to matter to you, besides how you lived your own life — whether it's while you're still on your deathbed, or when you stand in front of God. I decided a long time ago that I don't want to have any regrets when I look back at this time that we spent together as a family. I want my child to know that I did everything humanly possible to point them toward Christ and Heaven. You will want to do that as well. The time goes quick, and there's not much room for error, but if you give it your all it will be extremely rewarding for you.

I heard a thought-provoking story awhile back about a man in prison who was placed in a padded cell because he had attempted to end his own life. He was visited by a pastor, who asked him what had brought him to this low point in his life. The man explained that he was a money manager who had betrayed people's trust and cheated many out of their life's savings. He explained that he knew what he had done was wrong, and deserved to spend most of the rest of his life in prison. That is not why he had tried to commit suicide. The part that he could not face was that his son had always looked up to him. His son was always at his side and wanted to be wherever his father was.

As he grew older, his son learned the family business and eventually realized his dream of becoming his father's partner. When the arrests came, his son was arrested with him and would be spending much of the rest of his life in prison as well. The memory of this—leading his son in the wrong direction with irreversible circumstances—was more than the man could handle. As bad as that potentially true story sounds, it does have a higher moral. If a person were to find themselves in Hell someday, as horrible as that would be, how much more tragic would it be if their children ended up following them there too?

Chapter Four

THE LESS TRAVELED ROAD

*O*ne of my goals as I set out to write this book was to help parents discover that there really is a way to direct your child's life toward God, and away from Hell. It's not down the normally traveled path; it's not noticeable, worn or well marked; it's not obvious at all. If anything, it's all but hidden.

I stumbled on it myself, but truth be told, I'm sure God directed me toward it without me even knowing. In order to lead my daughter down that path, I had to first, and at the same time—kind of like on-the-job training—fix my own spiritual problem. I mentioned earlier that if you have to ask the question, "Should I get my baby baptized?" then you may have to do a little spiritual evaluation in your own life in order to see where you stand. Once you examine own your situation in the light of God's Word, you may find the need for a little renovation in order to lead your child properly.

There are a couple quick tests you can take to help see where you stand spiritually. The first is to answer the question, "If you were to die today, would you go to Heaven?" The common answers I get when I ask that question are, "I am a pretty good person, so hopefully the good things I do will out weigh the bad," or

"I hope so." Neither of these is the answer you want your children to give someday, because this answer is not the answer of a person who is Heaven-bound. If you answered, "Hopefully the good things I do will out weigh the bad," how could you ever really be sure you had done enough good? Maybe you did 999 things right but needed to do one thousand. Maybe you lost count and thought you did one thousand. Maybe it's 10 thousand that are needed. Who knows? How could you ever really be sure what the magic number is?

If you answered, "I hope so," then it is clear that you're really not sure what it would take to enter Heaven, but you're hoping that whatever it is, you may have done it. The answer to the question, "Will you go to Heaven when you die?" has got to be yes. If you're not sure, it's not going to happen. Jesus says pointblank in the Bible that in order to enter Heaven, He has to know you and you have to know Him. That means that in your lifetime you will have to start a relationship with Him. How else will you get to know each other?

That leads us to the second spiritual test question, "Have you ever started a personal relationship with Jesus Christ?" I am convinced that you would not be reading this book unless you wanted to give your child the very best chance in this life, as well as throughout eternity. In order to do that, you are going to have to learn to follow Jesus yourself. There is no other way. If you try to lead your child to Jesus while you are only pretending to follow Him, your child will know and eventually take a different path.

So, first things first—you have got to get right with God. It's a very simple process and only requires a choice. You have to make the choice to follow Him from this day forth. Once you make that decision, a flood of peace will wash over you. For many people though, it's not quite that simple. Deep down they're not really sure they even believe in God. To me, that is understandable. If you have never seen God do anything in your life that you are sure could only have been God doing it, then in order to believe, you have to go on somebody else's say so. That can be hard to do. There are other possibilities though that may help. For one, carefully read the four Gospels in the Bible starting with the book of John. If you do not have a Bible, you can read these books online for free. If you go to biblegateway.com, you can even choose the Bible translation you want to use. The book of John and the other three Gospels will help you understand exactly who Jesus was and what He did for you.

Many, many people turn to God once they read about Jesus without ever seeing any other proof of God's existence first. The life of Jesus as told in these four books (Matthew, Mark, Luke and John) has been an accepted historical fact for nearly two thousand years, so you can trust these accounts to be true. Jesus is the part of God that you can see and understand. Once you accept Him as your Savior, all the other pieces of the puzzle will slowly fall into place. While you are reading these four Bible books, some of the more important things that you should notice are as follows:

1. Jesus was God in human flesh.

God miraculously placed Himself in a virgin's womb to be born as a man and live on the earth. The prophet Isaiah said He would be called Immanuel, which means God with us. Because He was not conceived in the natural way, He did not contract the sin that comes from human parents, and so He way holy (pure; sinless).

2. Jesus is the Creator of all things.

Jesus is the Creator of the heavens and the earth and all that is in them. He spoke all things into existence according to His will and holds all things together by His power. He is the Creator, giver, and sustainer of all life. It would pay for you to take a closer look at creation. The earth, the universe, and even life itself all points to a Divine Creator. The Bible says that all things were made by Jesus (John 1:3). As you study creation, it becomes perfectly clear that there is nothing that could have happened by chance or accident, and the Biblical account is the only possible truth.

3. Jesus is the Lamb of God.

Throughout the Old Testament of the Bible, God developed the idea of sacrificing a spotless lamb to pay for sin. These lambs were temporary sacrifices and did not provide for forgiveness throughout eternity, but only for the present. Jesus was sent to be the perfect, spotless, sinless Lamb that would be sacrificed to make a permanent payment for the sins of all who will trust in Him.

4. Jesus performed miracles.

It is true that several people in the Bible did miracles by God's empowerment. However, Jesus performed certain miracles that only the Messiah could do. They were one, to give sight to a person blind from birth; two, to cast out a mute demon; three, to raise a person from the dead who had been dead for four days; and four, to heal a person with leprosy. Not only did Jesus do these four things, but the book of John states, "There are many other things Jesus did. If every one of them were written down, I suppose the whole world would not be big enough for all the books that would be written" (John 21:25).

5. Jesus taught people how to live right.

Up until the time of Christ, the world in general had a very different approach to interaction with others. Jesus introduced concepts that were not common, and I suspect if the world had been left to its own and Jesus had not come, it probably would have self-destructed long ago. Imagine a world with no peacemakers, no charities, no forgiveness, no real rules or laws. The biggest, meanest people are in charge. Raping, stealing, killing, pillaging. There are actually places like that in the world today. They are the very places that do not allow the teachings of Jesus Christ. He taught people the guidelines for living right. He had the words that give life to the hearer.

6. Jesus is the Way, the Truth, and the Life.

When the apostle Thomas asked Jesus how they could know the way to get to the place where He was going, Jesus told him, "I am the Way..." According to Jesus, the One who created Heaven, there is no other way to enter it than to go through Him. He is the door by which we must enter. He taught that in order to use Him as the door, all we have to do is put our faith and trust in Him. We can safely do this because He went on to tell Thomas that He was also the Truth — the absence of all lies — and the Life. If we put our trust in Him, we may enter Heaven through Him and stay with Him forever. He is the Giver of our earthly life and offers an eternal extension to all who believe.

7. Jesus is the Savior of the world.

The Bible teaches that because of sin, all people are lost and headed for Hell. Hell is the death penalty for our sin. By sending Jesus Christ, God offered a way for us to be pardoned from that debt. It required that His perfect, sinless Son must be crucified on the cross at Calvary. The death of Jesus could be used as a substitute payment for our sin. His death gives us an option as to whether we would like to pay for our sin with our own death in Hell, or use the death of Jesus to pay for it instead. If we decide to trust in Christ's death as payment for our sin, we can have life in Heaven forever. Because He gave His life to pay the penalty for mankind's sin, He is the Savior of the world.

8. Jesus rose from the dead.

Although Jesus was crucified to death and buried in a tomb, three days later He rose from the dead. In so doing, He demonstrated a number of things. One is that God has power over death and can raise people from the dead as He chooses. Another is that by rising from the dead, Jesus proved that His claims to have power over sin and death were true. In fact, rising from the dead should prove beyond any shadow of doubt that everything He ever said was true.

9. Jesus ascended into Heaven.

Forty days after Jesus rose from the dead, while He was with His followers on the Mount of Olives, Jesus ascended into Heaven. He had previously told His followers that He would be going back to Heaven to prepare a place for them. He didn't just vanish, leaving them to wonder if He really had gone back to heaven. He actually rose off the ground into the sky as they watched until He was out of sight.

10. Jesus is coming again.

This is the event that all true believers are waiting for. When Jesus returns, He will gather together all of the people who have put their faith and trust in Him. When Jesus told His disciples that He was going to Heaven to prepare a place for them, He did not stop there. He also said that He would be coming back to get them. The Bible teaches that this includes all those who put their faith and trust in His life, death, burial, and resurrection. If He is your Savior, then He will be taking you with Him.

These are just ten of the things you should notice as you read through the books of Matthew, Mark, Luke, and John. We call these books the four Gospels because the word "gospel" means good news. As you read through this list of only ten of the many things that these four books teach us about Jesus, it seems pretty obvious why they call it the Good News.

You should also discover from your reading that starting a personal relationship with Jesus is essential and not all that difficult. It actually only requires a few minutes in conversation with God to bring the whole thing about. You simply need to tell God that you understand your sin is keeping you apart from Him and will eventually lead you to the place called Hell. Tell Him you believe that He sent Jesus to die for you and that you would like to have the death of Jesus become a substitute payment for your sin so that you can be set free from this debt you owe.

Once you pray these things and believe that God has done them for you, at that moment Jesus becomes your Savior and you are saved from your sins. It really is that simple. The Bible says that your name is now written down in Heaven and you are a permanent citizen there. The next step then is to start living like a child of God. God's Spirit will help you do that. The main thing is to try not to repeat the mistakes you have made in the past, but learn how God would like you to live from this moment forward and then strive for that. This is the course of action you must take if you are going to effectively lead your child in the right direction.

> You should not stay away from the church meet-ings, as some are doing, but you should meet together and encourage each other. Do this even more as you see the day coming
> ~Hebrews 10:25

Another thing that would be very beneficial to your spiritual growth is to find a Bible-believing church to attend. God is mightily involved in churches that honor Him. It can be hard to know which church would be the right one, but you already have one big clue. Any church that promotes christening babies or sprinkling adults should probably be avoided. I say that for a number of reasons — some of which I have already mentioned — but also because there are so many variables and so much uncertainty surrounding what is scriptural and what is manmade, you will end up wasting your time. It is very hard to stay focused on the goal of learning to know Christ when you are surrounded by uncertainty.

Therefore, you will have to use wisdom when you make complicated choices like choosing the right church.

In my book, *Which God Should I Choose?* I have a section dedicated to helping you clearly understand God's work in Creation, as well as finding a God-honoring, Bible-believing church. It is imperative for the welfare of your child (or children and family) that you do not compromise on the issue of finding a true Bible-believing church. After all, if you are going to take this step, why would you want to risk bringing your family into a negative environment when Godly churches are still available?

One way that helps when trying to decide on proper church procedures is to go back in history and find out how the first century Christians conducted their church business. Much of that can be derived directly from the Bible. Be advised — I did not say the early church. By early church, I mean the later second and third century church. The first century church would be the Apostles and their audience. We have to realize that there is a big difference between the two when we're talking about the first century church (Apostles) and the early church (second and third century — after the Apostles and first believers were mostly dead). There is a lot of information concerning the doctrines (teachings) of the early church (second and third century), and we can see clearly that much of it had strayed from sound Biblical teaching and looks more like modern day religions rather than the first century Christian church.

The first century Christians tried to imitate Christ. That's why they were named Christians in the first place. They placed a high emphasis on trusting that Jesus was the Savior of their souls. Consequently, they taught that a changed life should accompany their faith in Christ. This is why they tried to imitate Him. This wasn't a hypocritical lip service imitation — preaching one thing and doing another — but a genuine response to a genuine conversion. Instead of hatred for others, including their enemies, they now loved one another; instead of being filled with anger, they were now peaceful; instead of holding grudges, they were now forgiving; instead of being greedy, they were now generous — especially with the poor and needy; instead of being immoral, they were now trying to live pure lives; instead of being enemies of God, they were now trying to live like His friends. Finding people capable of completely living this way is impossible, but we should be searching for a church where people are at least consistently *trying* to live this way.

As we study the first century church, we see that they did not christen infants. Nowhere in the Bible is an infant seen being baptized. There are instances of whole households believing and being baptized, but there is no mention of infants or even children. And, as discussed earlier, an infant would be incapable of believing. Although there are plenty of arguments that support infant baptism, such as the "whole household" of the Philippian jailer, it is still purely speculation and truly does not fit the message of salvation — which is, again, to believe in Jesus and be baptized. The Greek word translated "believe" means more than just acknowledge His existence. It carries the meaning of trusting in Him, depending on Him, relying on Him, and adhering to Him. When you come to that belief, it is the time to be baptized. From the perspective of early church history, there is plenty of evidence that infant baptism really didn't become an accepted practice until after 200 AD. One of the earliest references to infant baptism is by a man named Tertullian, who was considered to be an early church father. He argued that it was not logical

48

to baptize an infant because they could not believe in (trust in, depend on, rely on, or adhere to) Jesus, and Tertullian wondered why then "the sponsors (infants) likewise should be thrust into danger..."[1]

I have to tell you — that's one of the things that would have been on my mind if I had decided to go through with a christening. My daughter weighed seven pounds and was twenty inches long when she was born. She could lie on my forearm while I was feeding her. It may have caused a hostage situation if somebody tried to take her from me and thrust her under water at that age and size. Tertullian, in fact, was right to be concerned about the welfare of a baby during this process. He probably had heard of infants drowning during christenings back then, just as infants have drowned during recent times while being baptized. Besides drowning, there certainly are many other health risks to consider anytime you submerge a baby under water. Unless it's running water, imagine the germs that can live in a tub of public water.

The health department advises against taking a canned beverage out of a tub of ice water that others have dipped their hands in. They also advise against letting children dunk for apples anymore because they now know of the germs that can spread from one kid to the next through the dunking water. Imagine immersing your infant into it.

As you read through this book, you will see that — just as Tertullian and countless others down through the ages have agreed — there is absolutely no spiritual reason for christening a baby.

Concerning older children, Tertullian also stated, "The Lord does indeed say, 'Forbid them not to come unto me.' Let them 'come,' then, while they are growing up; ... let them become Christians when they have become able to know Christ." That certainly is sound wisdom from one of the earliest known church officials to address the subject. Although children of any age being baptized are not mentioned in the Bible, the Bible does make it clear that anyone who truly understands and believes in Christ's blood as atonement for their sin should not be hindered from being baptized. That would definitely include children who are old enough to understand completely and believe.

The Greek word "baptizo" would also apply here and mean baptism by immersion. In fact, whenever water baptism is mentioned in the Bible, it is understood to be baptism by immersion. The Greek word used in the Bible when speaking of baptism is the Greek word "baptizo." Although there are other words used in other instances of religious washing, this is the only word used in the Bible when referring to what we are talking about here—water baptism of a person who believes in Christ. According to Strong's Greek Dictionary, as well as all other reliable, accepted Greek dictionaries, "baptizo," in the original Greek, means "immerse or submerge ... cover wholly with fluid." It never means sprinkle, dip, or pour.

If we're going to become Christians (imitators of Christ), wouldn't it make sense to be baptized like Jesus was baptized? When Jesus was baptized by John the Baptist, the Bible says, "As soon as Jesus was baptized, he came up out of the water" (Mathew 3:16).

Mark 1:9 says that Jesus was baptized by John in the Jordan River. Now I'm not saying that you should be baptized in the Jordan River (although many are). I'm using these two verses to emphasize the point that if Jesus went into the Jordan River to be baptized (Greek word "baptizo") and came up out of the water after He was baptized, then wisdom, common sense, or even logic has got to convince you that baptism Biblically is by immersion.

I have heard it said that in certain instances — where a person is not able to get into the water to be baptized — pouring water over them would be okay. I'm not sure who would have the right to make that rule since it is not found in the Bible. If anyone asked my advice on this, I would say that if you are not able to get into water — whether it be health, physical ability, or whatever the case — It would probably be better to leave the baptism out. This would be the Scriptural advice as well, because when the thief who was being crucified on the cross next to Jesus confessed his belief in Him, Jesus told him that he would be with Him in Paradise that very day. Since this man was not afforded the luxury of being able to get down off the cross after his conversion to Christ and be baptized, and since he had his legs broken and died a short time later, he reinforced the rest of Scripture that teaches that we are saved by grace through faith alone and baptism is merely an outward display of our faith and obedience to Christ. God knows the ones who wish they could be baptized, but for very truthful and understandable reasons are not able to.

There are several other church leaders during the second and third centuries that spoke out both for and against infant baptism, as well as for and against baptism other than by immersion. It appears from history that infant christening and baptism by sprinkling, dipping, or pouring did not start in the Christian church until after the Apostles were all dead. If it had, the Apostles — the actual Bible writers — would have addressed the subject themselves. Although they were like firemen, constantly dowsing heresy fires that were popping up amongst the body of believers, they rarely tried to put out fires that weren't burning yet. Truthfully, I'll bet that they felt the teaching on this subject was undeniably crystal clear and that nobody could get it messed up. Just as truthfully, when you study it out, you find they really did do a good job explaining it all and it is undeniably crystal clear just the way it is written.

Chapter Five

MY BEAUTIFUL BABY

One of things that impresses is me is that, when considering whether to baptize your baby or not, it shows that you, as a parent, have a genuine concern for your child's future. Not just the foreseeable future, but when considering baptism, you must have eternity in view. Because you are seeking true answers to this hard question, I know you care about your baby and your baby's future, and that is commendable. A caring parent is rare these days. Your concern for your child's spiritual future is what prompted me to write this book. I cannot stand the thought of a parent truly wanting to see their child grow up to become part of God's family and be steered in the wrong direction. If you start out on the wrong road, how long will you follow it before you stop and ask directions? Maybe you're on the wrong road and don't know it. How far will you have to travel before you realize something's wrong?

As of 2013, I have been a spiritual leader of young people for eighteen years. You can trust my experience when I tell you that as a parent, you only have a small window of opportunity to make a spiritual impact on your child. If you get going too far in the wrong direction, even with a turn-around you likely will not have enough time left with them to undo the damage done once you begin their spiritual reconstruction. It's not impossible, but chances of success are far less great in these instances. It would behoove you to head off in the right direction from the start.

Among the hardest kids to reach for a true relationship with God are those who have been brought up in a religious atmosphere that includes infant baptism. Normally they only go through the motions and do what is required of them in order to please their parents or leaders, and at the same time are very suspicious of Biblical truth. They usually hang around true Bible programs (if they are ever introduced to one) for a short period of time and then are gone. As soon as they are old enough, they part company with all religious activity. In my observation, children who are raised by godly, Bible-believing parents are far more likely to follow the direction of their parents and develop a personal faith in God. However, much depends on the witness, testimony, and spiritual involvement of their parents as to how quickly and how strong they grow spiritually.

We will go step by step through the process that will help you raise your children in the teaching of the Lord. God actually does command parents to do this very thing and He gives stern warnings to those who choose not to. The horrible circumstances that children must cope with while they are growing up in the world today and the alarming numbers of children who cannot — cope, that is — should be all the warning we need. It's hard to believe it now, but within a few short years, that little bundle of joy you're holding in your arms is going to be heading off to pre-school. If you don't have this whole parenting thing down by then, you are not going to be prepared for the problems that have the potential to increase dramatically at that time.

Who has ever looked into their baby's eyes and thought, *I expect this baby to experience drugs in elementary school, become a rebellious teen, runaway, and end up on a milk carton somewhere – or in jail – whichever comes first?* It's just the opposite, isn't it? Aren't you thinking doctor, lawyer, football player, family business? Anything but juvenile delinquent! I mentioned before—the deck is stacked against you. In a blur, your baby will be a teenager. Your preparation work will be all but done by then and at that point either you will begin to enjoy the fruits of your hard work, or experience the bitter taste of failure and regret.

In order to substantiate what I am saying, I have compiled a handful of meaningful statistics that will help you get your mind around the urgent decisions that you are faced with. As I mentioned, I work with young people, and have for nearly two decades. In my opinion, these national statistics are either accurate, or possibly even a touch low. Although they represent teenagers—ages thirteen and up—it is important to note that the groundwork is completed and the foundation is laid for these kids in preschool.

Although you will be dreaming of having a loving and peaceful relationship with your child, one in five teenagers run away from home. Although you are hoping that your child will be a sober, respectful young person, 90 percent of all teenagers try alcohol. 40 percent of all teenagers drink alcohol on a regular basis and 30 percent of teenagers are binge drinkers. Although you expect to have a wise, health-conscience student, 19 percent of all twelfth graders smoke cigarettes. Although you are sure your child will just say no to drugs, over 36 percent of teens smoke marijuana, and although you would like your child to be truthful with you and confide in you with everything, 70 percent of all teenagers hide their online habits from their parents[2] and, even though it could not be possible for *your* child, nearly 9 percent of all teenage girls become pregnant[3] (that has to mean at least nearly an equal amount of boys are involved). As bad as all of that sounds, sadly, nearly 8 percent of all teenagers attempt suicide.[4]

As a parent, I am sure these are not your goals. Although I include the above warnings, this book is not about what your child could become, but what your child can become. My goal is not to scare you, but to teach you. God has given you this child, and He has given you the awesome opportunity and responsibility to raise that child — with His help — according to the teachings of the Lord. I was not aware of this when my daughter was born. I imagine you may not have been either. That's evidenced by the fact that both of us were trying to find out about christening.

Finding out the truth about God is a slow, lengthy process. The beauty of it is that every step of the way, God is with you, and as you take each step, you are as advanced in that knowledge as God wants you to be. In order to raise your child properly and end up with a grown child that honors you and brings you joy, you are going to have to learn a lot about God. It's okay that you don't know too much right now, because your baby doesn't either. But, as your baby progresses, your knowledge of God will have to progress as well, and you will have to always stay at least a couple steps ahead. Since your child is learning new things constantly, you are going to have to mirror that pace, not only to know what the next step spiritually is at every moment, but also in order to answer the tough questions that will begin shortly.

I'm getting a little ahead of myself here, but when my daughter was two years old, we were going through a huge tent at one of the biggest antique market events in New York State. The tent was packed elbow to elbow — or elbow to stroller in our case. It was slow going. My daughter was staring up at the tent roof from her vantage point in the stroller. All of a sudden she said in a loud voice, "Dad?"

There was silence in the tent all around me. "Yes, dear?" I asked quietly.

"Is God everywhere?" she asked in that same loud voice.

I smiled. Everybody nearby was waiting for my answer. "Yes, dear, He is."

She pondered that answer for a second, and then asked with a questioning look, "Even in this tent?"

I smiled bigger. She was getting it. "Yes, dear, even in here," I answered.

That satisfied her curiosity for the time being, but those are two-year-old questions. The older they get, the harder the questions get. If we can't answer them, then they are going to turn to their friends, or worse, the Internet — and from the heresy that I see all over the Internet, it will not take much to confuse your child and head them down the wrong road fast.

In fact, I have had to field all kinds of crazy questions from all kinds of kids over the years. Most of them have either heard something or devised their own conclusions and aren't so much asking me, but explaining to me what they believe. Once they get fallacy in their heads, it's nearly impossible to shake it out. It is far better to fill their heads with truth and keep it filled so they will recognize the false teachings when they come. That's why I say you have to start learning now, before they start learning. You have to be their spiritual leader. You won't be able to trust anybody else to do that. Just assume there is nobody. There's probably not anyway.

You're it. You're the one God called for this. It is His plan and desire for you to teach your child about Him.

But where do you start? Actually, you may be starting right where I started. Since you are questioning the validity of baptizing infants, you may even be a little bit ahead of where I was. I went in search of someone to christen my daughter. Actually, I sent my wife. That's what men do. She told me there was a minister that came through the hardware store where she worked almost every day. "Get him," was my reply. After a couple days, she did. She approached him at work and made arrangements for him to stop at our house one evening after supper.

In order to teach our children the truth about God, we have to first learn it for ourselves. I did not realize how little I knew about God until I met with the reverend that night. Anything I had learned from the few Bible studies I had participated in or the church services I had attended over the years had morphed into my own personal understanding of what I thought God was, or should be. The God that was portrayed to me at this "meeting" was nothing like the God I had conjured up in my mind, but the reverend had Bible verses ready to substantiate everything he was telling us. I remember going away from that encounter thinking that this man knew more about God and the Bible than anyone I could ever remember meeting.

It impressed me so much — not just the thought that he knew so much about God and the Bible, but that it was actually possible for someone to know that much about them — that I decided right then and there, I needed to find these things out for myself. I discovered that there were actually circles of people that I was completely unaware of that knew all of the things that this reverend knew, and even more. At that time,

I had no clue about the wealth of knowledge that God had planned to reveal to me. So that's where it begins then. You have to erase the slate that holds all of your misconceptions about God and start fresh. Plus, you have to be willing to give 100 percent toward this effort of learning the truth about God so you can teach your child properly.

The first thing I wanted to learn, since I was starting over, was what the Bible was trying to teach me. What was the bottom line? I really liked what I saw in the people who knew about God, but what drove them? I started at the beginning. Learning who Jesus was, why He lived, and why He died. That is for sure the place you must start. Once you learn these things, everything else will naturally fall into place.

Chapter Six

THE BOTTOM LINE

Someone has said, what matters most in life is what we do with Jesus Christ. I guess in order to know what to do with Jesus Christ, you would first have to know for sure who He is, and/or who He represents. A clear understanding of Jesus Christ will also be crucial as you raise your child to follow Him. After all, He is the one that the baptism that you were considering for your baby in the first place represents. Baptism is a declaration of faith in Jesus Christ and His death, burial, and resurrection.

In order to know anything, the best place to start is usually at the beginning. When thinking about going back to the beginning, I am always reminded of the comedy routines where people are asked to start at the beginning and immediately they go back to their birth and pick up the story from there. Although the story of Jesus Christ in the Bible actually goes back beyond His birth to the creation of the Earth and the heavens — and even prior to that, eternity past — we can get a clear understanding of who He is by starting at His birth. Before Jesus was born in Bethlehem, there was plenty of talk recorded in the Old Testament concerning the coming of a Savior. This Savior would be the spiritually anointed (blessed or set apart) One (Christ or Messiah) of God and would be sent by God to free mankind from sin and death and lead the hearts of the people of the world back to God.

Seven hundred years before Jesus was born, the prophet Isaiah wrote that a virgin would give birth to a Son and He would be called Immanuel, which means "God with us." A little over two thousand years ago, the angel Gabriel visited a virgin girl named Mary who lived in Nazareth and told her that she would conceive and bear a Son. She questioned this only because she had never had sexual relations with a man. The angel explained that God would place the baby in her womb supernaturally. Because the baby was not conceived by natural processes, He did not inherit mankind's sin. As Isaiah had said, the mother was a virgin and the baby was Immanuel — God with us — God in human flesh.

The angel also told Mary that His name would be Jesus. Since Mary was a Hebrew girl, she likely spoke Hebrew. In Hebrew, the name Jesus would be Yeshua. Yeshua translated into English means "Savior" or "God's salvation." So, not only was Jesus born to a virgin so that He would not have a sin-infected body, He was also God with us, because God had placed Himself in Mary's womb to be born in human form (Immanuel), as well as named God's Savior (Yeshua) and Messiah (Christ).

Jesus Christ then is more than just a name; it is in, reality, who He is. His name says that He is the Savior (Yeshua — Jesus) set apart and blessed as God's Messiah (Christ). He is God in human flesh (Immanuel — God with us). Once you come to the realization that Jesus Christ is the One God sent to be the Savior of the world and that He was in fact God in a human body, it makes deciding what to do with Him that much easier. Assuming that your child will stumble onto this truth by accident is a bit delusional. The greatest hope they have of finding it is through your direction. It is essential then that you help them find it. They have to, because the alternative is Hell throughout eternity. For me, I care as much about my child not being in Hell as I care about myself not being there.

The Bible teaches that each one of us was placed on the earth for a certain purpose. Whether we realize that purpose in our own lifetime or not depends on the choice we make with Jesus Christ. Pilate asked the people what they wanted to do with Jesus. Their choice was, "Crucify Him!" Unfortunately (for them), they were giving the command for the event that would allow all people from then on who believe in Him to have their sin pardoned, while they themselves — as unbelievers — would remain responsible for the penalty due for their sin, which is eternal death in Hell. Turning your back on Him now yields basically the same result. Following Him at this point will not only allow you to reap the benefits of knowing Christ as Savior, but will potentially help your child as well.

Jesus Christ was sent by God to replace the lambs that had been sacrificed regularly for the sins of the people since the time of Moses. Temporary sacrifices would no longer be needed or accepted. Jesus was called the Lamb of God that takes away the sin of the world. In order to do that, He would have to be sacrificed for sin in much the same way the sacrificial lambs were. The lamb sacrifices brought temporary forgiveness for their owner's sin while the sacrifice that Jesus made of His life brings a permanent cleansing from sin for all who believe in what He did for them.

By declaring that you believe in Jesus, you are saying that you believe that the sacrifice of His life that He made on the cross at Calvary was all that was needed to be done in order to pay the penalty for your sin and cleanse you from it. You believe that all your past, present. and future sins have been forgiven and you now have been given the right to be called a child of God. You believe that because of the sacrifice that Jesus Christ made, you will be able to spend eternity in Heaven as an heir of God and co-heir with Jesus Christ, and nothing can take that from you. You are now trusting in Him completely for all of that. That is what you are saying you believe when you put your faith in Jesus Christ. If you really mean it, you have met the only Biblical requirement to make it be so. With that in mind, life now takes on a whole different perspective. At this point you are now a new creation in Christ. It is time to start over with a new life, a new purpose, and a new direction. You can now start rebuilding your life according to what God wants you to do. He will not make you do this on your own either. When you put your faith in Him, He sends His Spirit to live with you and help you gain self control over your sinful desires. Without His help, it would be impossible.

I did this same thing after my meeting with the reverend that night (who turned out to be a Bible-believing pastor). I now saw a way to raise my daughter that was previously unavailable to me. It wasn't christening that I needed to get for her, but a new direction in *my* life. I prayed to God and told Him that I had tried to do things my way for my entire life. It seemed like the summation of my life so far was failure. I was now ready to do things His way, and I asked Him for His help.

Once you do this, it's time to find a Bible-believing church. It's important to understand right from the start that there is no perfect church. Churches — even ones that base their faith on the Bible — are populated by people, and people oftentimes disappoint one another. The beauty of a true Bible-believing church, though, is the love in Christ that the parishioners share, and the sincere desire they have to forgive one another when misunderstandings arise, as well as overlooking one another's shortcomings. God does command believers to join together in church settings. Besides learning more about Him at these meetings, there are also the benefits of the love, help, and encouragement that only a Bible-believing church family can give.

It's also important to understand that people in a church may not have reached the high standard that we are seeking to obtain, so our eyes should not be set on their level. We should have our eyes fixed on Christ. That is the goal we should be aiming for. That is who we should be comparing ourselves to. We do not want to let ourselves be bothered by what the people around us are thinking so much as what Christ is thinking. Is He pleased with our actions and our attitudes? Are we living like Christ when others around us are failing to do so? Is He happy with the attitudes we display when others disappoint us or try to bring us down? It is a high standard, but when we realize that many of the people around us are struggling to reach it themselves, it can help us be more understanding of and less frustrated with their actions.

While finding a Bible-believing church will help you develop socially as a Christian, it is also vitally important for you to develop personally as well. This will be accomplished by routine Bible reading and prayer. The Bible is God's Word. It is one of the ways God uses to help you grow in His grace and knowledge. It is extremely important that—as a follower of Christ—you find a way to read at least a little bit in your Bible every day. Daily Bible devotions are essential to Christian growth.

You should make plans to set apart some time for Bible reading each day. If you are new at it, or haven't spent all that much time in the Bible, it would be advisable to start out by reading the Gospel of John. This book will help you solidify in your mind the things you now know to be true about Jesus. Also, a solid daily devotional such as Our Daily Bread® will help get you started every day. Our Daily Bread© is a free publication, or is also available online at rbc.org. Another equally handy tool for daily Bible study is the Word of Life Quiet Time Diary© with commentary, which is available through Word of Life Fellowship, Inc (wol.org).

There are, of course, a number of good daily devotionals to choose from, but I caution you that not all of them are scripturally sound, so make sure that you do your homework and only acquire a daily devotional from a known-to-be reputable organization. The ones I have mentioned here are true to God's Word and reliably accurate. It would pay to at least start with these, and then as you become more acclimated with God's truth, you can branch out from there. Probably what will work best is to set your alarm a little earlier than usual and do your Bible reading first, because once the day gets going, "later" oftentimes never comes. It is also helpful to pray before you start and ask God to help you understand what you will be reading that day. As hard as it is to understand at first, the Bible is living and powerful. It has the power to change lives. As you study it, your life will transform.

Another way to reach a better understanding of God is through prayer. Prayer is simply carrying on a conversation with God. Again, there is certainly more than one right way or one right time to pray. Some people use an acronym such as A.C.T.S. to help them stay focused in prayer.

A: Adoration. Tell God how great you know Him to be.

C: Confession. Even though God forgave your sin at salvation, you still sin every day and need to confess (admit) that to God.

T: Thanksgiving. Thank God for everything you can think of, because He provided it all.

S: Supplication. This means asking God for what you need and — more importantly — asking God to give others you know what they need.

Is there a right time to pray? The Apostle Paul says to pray continually. This can mean living in an attitude of prayer, talking to God throughout the day, asking for advice, thanking Him for different things, and praising His intervention in your life. It would be good as well to set a specific time each day to get together with your family members and pray. Perhaps after dinner or just before bed might work best for this "official" time for prayer.

Chapter Seven

CURRENT AFFAIRS

Once we get our personal spiritual affairs in order with God — which I am hoping you have by now taken care of — the necessity to get our family's spiritual affairs straightened out becomes much more apparent. Chances are you and your spouse will not catch the vision of turning to God at the same moment. It happens sometimes, but usually one or the other will get saved first and then lead the other one to Christ. I would suggest reading this book together. Possibly out loud, taking turns reading to each other. The more you can do together devotionally as a family, the stronger your family bond will grow.

You might also consider having your spouse read my book, *Which God Should I Choose?* which will help them know for sure that there is only one true God, and that He has a plan and purpose for their life. Once they know for sure that God is real, it will become more urgent for them to make a personal decision. Whether your spouse is on board at the moment or not, the welfare of your baby's spiritual future is no less important and you will have to start almost immediately making critical decisions. For the most part, whoever raises your baby will have a hand in swaying their spiritual convictions. If you use childcare or babysitters, whatever their lifestyle portrays is what your baby will begin to mimic. No one is going to care for your baby's spiritual future like you do.

If your parents or your spouse's parents are unsaved, whatever is in their home is what is going to enter your baby's mind. Whatever they talk about, whatever is on their television, and whatever music they listen to. All of this will enter your baby's mind, which is — and always will be — like a sponge, absorbing whatever it comes in contact with. It is unadvisable then to use any secular daycare or babysitter. By secular, I mean worldly or unsaved; having no concern for the true God. Your child is young and impressionable. You have to ask yourself what you want them to be impressed with. If your babysitter shows up littered with piercings or is suction cupped to a cell phone or iPod, it doesn't take much imagination to envision your child's future.

If you take a casual approach to this critical decision, things are going to spiral out of hand pretty fast. If you doubt it, visit a secular childcare center or public preschool while your child is still a baby and observe the behavioral problems of the children present. How do the odds look for these children if they continue in the direction they are headed to eventually — accidentally — find their way to God? They're only about three years ahead of your child. The chances of finding a God-honoring individual to baby-sit for you on a regular, daily basis is slim, so the best advice would be to plan on raising your child yourself.

This would be sound Biblical advice as well, since the Bible does not command us to find someone else to raise our child, but is quite adamant about us raising our children ourselves. Referring to the teachings of God, Deuteronomy chapters four and six command us to, "Teach them to your children, and talk about them when you sit at home and walk along the road, when you lie down and when you get up" (Deuteronomy 6:7). In other words, always. We are also told, "Command your children to obey carefully everything in these teachings" (Deuteronomy 32:46). Furthermore, the Apostle Paul warns. "Fathers, do not make your children angry, but raise them with the training and teaching of the Lord" (Ephesians 6:4).

I'm not sure where the philosophy comes from that says even though we desired to be parents, once we are, it's okay to hand the child we so longed for off to somebody else for their upbringing. No matter how good the reasons may be, I contend that there is nothing that could be worth more than the soul of your child. And that is exactly what is at stake here. There is no job, career, or unfulfilled ambition that could possibly be worth the torment of seeing your child growing up to despise you—and worse, to despise God.

I imagine you would not consider taking your life savings and placing them as a bet at a gambling casino. However, leaving your child's spiritual future to chance will be much the same as carrying their soul into a casino and placing it down as a bet. Just like you would sooner protect your life savings and try your best to invest it wisely, never risking it on gambles, you should take the same guarded approach with your child's soul—leaving nothing to chance—investing in its future wisely and guarding it with your life.

Once you realize that at least one parent should stay at home and raise your child, it is time to start thinking about preschool. It is the next step, and it will be on you before you know it. If you took my dare and visited a secular preschool, then you're already fully aware that this is not the environment you want your

71

child learning in. Although many Christian schools offer preschool classes, it wouldn't be a bad idea at all to have your baby's preschool training at home. If you go online, there are plenty of Christian home preschool curriculums to choose from. There are many benefits to be gained by taking this course of action. Christian home preschool curriculum includes opportunities for your child to learn more about Jesus and the Bible. This will help to reinforce what you have been teaching all along. It also helps teach your child that they must learn from you, and not others. Since by then you will have been attending a Bible-believing church and reading your Bible every day for some time, you should feel much more qualified to handle this task. It may not seem like it at first, but even if you don't think you'll be able to do a good enough job, it will still be better than what your child could learn anywhere else.

When my daughter was born, I was not aware of the existence of Christian schools or home school. The life I lived was far removed from such things. After meeting with the pastor that first night about christening, my wife and I had agreed to meet once a week with him for beginner Christian lessons. This included a simple Bible lesson that included verbal quiz questions. One night the pastor found himself double booked. He and his wife had made plans to meet with a family for a time of fellowship around a lakeside campfire. Rather than cancel, he offered to have us come down to this lake home and have our lesson around the campfire there. It seemed a little awkward, but who could resist a setting like that? It turned out to be one of those life-changing events where you have to wonder, "What would have happened if I hadn't gone?"

The people who owned the cabin were very gra-cious hosts and it turned out that they had their grandchildren visiting them that week, so they were sitting out around the fire as well. I have to admit that I did not know it was possible for such children to exist. They were well-behaved, respectful, and as the Pastor asked the questions from the Bible quiz sheet, these kids — less than ten years old — knew all the answers. It was very impressive and a true eye-opening experience. As amazed as I was at that, after the lesson and quiz time was over, the children started singing Christian songs in harmony. I ascertained that they had learned all of these things in a Christian school. I went away from that campfire a changed man with a new purpose. That night I became aware for the first time that it was possible to raise a child like that and I became determined to see it through. I just had to learn how first. My daughter was three months old at that point, so basically it was on-the-job training for me.

Prior to preschool you will have a few years of quality education time with your child that when you look back, those years will be among your fondest memories. When my daughter was a baby, I would get up an hour and a half before work, go downstairs, make a cup of coffee, and then climb in a recliner for my daily Bible time. Every morning I would hear a thump on the floor above me and then see my baby daughter climbing and sliding her way down the stairs. At the bottom she would run across the room, jump up in the chair with me, and lay there on my arm while I read my Bible passages for the day. Within a short period of time I found a daily Bible devotional for toddlers (which was mostly picture coloring) and we would spend those early mornings together doing our Bible devotions before I left for work. Most nights, if we weren't at church, I would read to her, making sure to show her the words as I read. I could see her eyes following along, not understanding, but following.

By the time she turned three years old though, she was reading the books to me. At that point, I was able to get her a Bible devotional for school-age children that she was able to handle pretty well. Today, she spends more time in her Bible devotions than I do. That training began before preschool. It is never too soon to start. When she was a couple months old I remember we would dress her in a thing called a onesie. When we were out at night I would hold her up in her onesie, point toward the moon, and say, "See that honey? That's the moon. God made the moon." That may sound a little crazy, but today she has no doubt who made the moon.

You will soon have to start thinking about kindergarten and school as well. These decisions may be a little more difficult to make since most of us never dreamed we might someday be called upon by God to become a teacher. Christian school is an option, but may not be the best opportunity of the three main choices you will be faced with. In the opinion of many, public school should not be a consideration. It's going to boil down to how God leads you, but there are going to be enough problems in your child's life without subjecting them to the shortcomings of the secular education system. If you were considering baptism for a specific spiritual result in your child's life, you are not going to be happy with the finished product you receive back after twelve years in a public school.

I have heard plenty of couples reason that they are sending their kids into the public school system to evangelize the other children. That's like sending a sheep into a cave to rehabilitate the wolves that live there. It is rarely a good idea, and at best a gamble. I'm afraid I have to mention it again, but I have been working with public school children for a very long time and so I can say with certainty that this is one of those instances where you will find that you have chosen to fill a cup that has no bottom. As I think about it, I wouldn't know where to start if I were going to inform you of the wrong things that a child will learn in public school. State-run schools are anti-God and pro everything else.

I have to assume that the majority of you who are reading this have access to the Internet. I encourage you to do a little research into what school kids are talking about with one another on the different social websites. If the idea were to find a society of children that chased after the exact opposite of every godly principal in the Bible, you will have to exclaim, "I found it!" Many years ago I was relating to a Christian missionary friend who was home on leave how I had been sharing Christ with a group of teenagers weekly for a couple of years, but because of the lifestyles they were involved in, they just weren't responding. He thought about it for a moment and said, "Maybe you will have to consider them a lost generation and start with younger aged kids."

At first I was not willing to even consider that, but as I look back, to my knowledge only four or five of the hundred or so kids I worked with ten years ago are following the Lord today, and those were either home schooled or went to a Christian school. Since then I have learned that 50% of all born again Christians have accepted Christ before they were thirteen years old. Because of that, even though I work with teens still today, I also work with many preteens as well.

In many cases, well-meaning parents don't want to make the sacrifice that would be required in order to afford a Christian school or—for whatever reason they can come up with—they don't want to educate their child themselves, so they send their kids to public school. Sometimes it's for other reasons, like having interaction with other kids or better opportunities to play in organized sports. If social interaction is a concern, public school is not the answer. If children act like Christians in school, they will become social outcasts. They will oftentimes be ridiculed and picked on. To counter this, they may try to blend and will soon be converted to whatever the opposite of following God looks like.

As far as sports, I can't imagine that learning to play a sport better for a few years is worth the damage that can be done to a child's soul. No matter how good or talented the best sports star is, if they're running away from God, they will not be running in Heaven. All Christian schools have some kind of sports program that can help prepare a child for whatever sports they will be playing after they're eighteen years old, so it's not the greatest excuse to begin with. In most cases there are no sports after high school, and in best cases it will be a church softball league. There are also plenty of other kids to hang around with even in a small Christian school, so learning social skills, if anything, will be easier.

If a better education is a concern, it is a well documented fact that on average, home school and Christian school children receive higher national test scores than public school children.

If you are in fact not able to afford a private Christian school, there are still great options. Almost every area of the nation has home school organizations that bring groups of kids together regularly for sports and socialization. This is also an excellent opportunity for home school parents to get together to compare notes and share experiences.

You are not the same as those who do not believe. So do not join yourselves to them. Good and bad do not belong together. Light and darkness cannot share together.

~2 Corinthians 6:14

Chapter Eight

FIRST THINGS FIRST

*F*irst and foremost of things to consider is the heart of your child. You only have a few short years to introduce your child to God and lead them to Christ. You must understand that this cannot be accomplished by following a list of rules. Rules are very important— so important that we will take a look at some of the better ones in a bit—but not as important as the reasons for keeping them. Rules create structure in a child's life, and even though it may not seem like it at the time, they do appreciate them. The ones who grow up without rules are deep down the most miserable of all children. If rules are all there are, though, then you might as well raise a robot, because that will be what you end up with.

At some point, that robot is going to malfunction, because the things of the world will look much more enticing than the rules that keep your child from them. Your job will be to teach your child not to keep the rules because they have to, but to keep the rules because they want to. In order to want to keep the rules, first, of course, they have to make sense; and then second, they will have to prove to your child's heart that they have true worth. If the rules don't make sense and seem worthless, then a child may still keep them, but only because they have to. When you're not around or when they feel they're old enough to no longer be governed by your rules, then rules are not going to stop them from making bad decisions.

There are probably three main things that will help your children learn to want to keep the rules. Number one will be that they see that *you* want to keep the rules as well. If you can show your child that you have the freedom to do a lot of different things that they are not allowed to, but you don't do those things because they are wrong, your child will notice and be impressed. This can cover a variety of rules ranging anywhere from using alcohol to watching R rated movies. If you keep the rules you have for them, not because you have to, but because you want to, those rules will make a lot more sense to them. Of course, you will constantly have to remind them why you keep these rules and how important it is. They need to know all of the reasons for keeping rules and why it is so important for them that they make the right choices.

The second thing that will help them understand the importance of keeping rules is the unity that it creates with you, the parent. I do not agree at all with the philosophy that says you should not be friends with your children. If you are a wise, loving parent, your child is going to grow accustomed to that joy-filled relationship. When they do something wrong and are punished, the break from their happy bond with you will crush them. They won't understand at a young age all of the emotions that will overtake them after a spanking. For a youngster, a scolding and a quick light slap on the backside is all it takes to rock their world. After such an incident, my daughter would run to the couch, bury her head in her arms and cry. I would give her a minute and then go over and sit next to her. I'd say something like,

"Okay, honey, what happened…what went wrong?" I would make her explain to me as best she could what caused our unhappiness. It didn't take long for her to figure out that breaking rules caused disharmony. She learned at a very young age the importance of family unity and that it doesn't happen by breaking rules. Because she wanted that bond of friendship intact, she wanted to try to do what was right in our eyes.

The third thing—and most important—that will help a child learn to want to be obedient is because this is what God wants. If a child learns at a young age that the rules at home reflect the rules in the Bible, it creates a standard for them. If a child learns that rules like "don't lie" or "don't steal" aren't just rules that somebody made up for no good reason, but are rules that God designed and expects us to keep, they will be more inclined to keep them. You need to help your child come to the place where they say in their heart, "I want to live in a way that will please God. God's rules are my rules." I didn't really know that God made the rules and expected me to keep them until later in life. I kept the rules at a young age because of the threat to be put in a "home" if I didn't behave. I didn't know what a "home" was, but it sounded scary enough to keep me in line for awhile.

Years ago I was riding with a friend who had a daughter about ten years older than mine. I mentioned that I was concerned about a little stubborn streak I was seeing in my daughter and wondered if rebellion was right around the corner. He told me that he had gone through a very similar experience with his own daughter at eight years old. He found that when she got a little disobedient, setting her down and asking her what she supposed Jesus was thinking about all of this solved the problem. Because she was already well aware that Jesus was always with her—always watching, always expecting the best from her—she would immediately change her attitude.

I've only had to ask that question two or three times in the past ten years. It is amazing how important it is to a child who knows God personally to not be displeasing to Him. That's not surprising because it should be the same exact way for us. That's why we want to keep the rules—because it pleases God. Our children should be learning that from us. Our actions and attitudes should reflect our sincere desire to please God and our children should see it in us and understand it. They will only have that desire to keep the rules because they want to if they learn it from us. At some point soon it has to become their choice. It has to become the way they choose to live their lives. If it doesn't, then the only alternative is rebellion and rule breaking.

Hopefully you can see the importance of pointing your child's heart in the right direction. I doubt we'll ever know what would happen if you raised the same child in two different scenarios. If in one instance you raised a child to develop in their heart a desire to follow God, and in the second instance raised the same child in a home that doesn't follow God, would the same child—in the two different instances—have two completely different hearts? Would you have two completely different outcomes? As I say, I doubt we would ever really be able to figure something like that out for sure, but I do know that if you raise two *different* children in these two different scenarios that you will definitely have two children with completely different hearts. In at least most cases, one heart will be for God and the other will not.

Jesus said, "Good people bring good things out of the good they stored in their hearts. But evil people bring evil things out of the evil they stored in their hearts. People speak the things that are in their hearts" (Luke 6:45). Our job is to get the right things—the good things—in the hearts of our children. Obviously Jesus wasn't talking about the human organ that pumps blood throughout the body that we call a heart. He was talking about the innermost being of a person. When we say "with all my heart," we're talking about who we are—our soul and spirit. It's the part of us that lives in our flesh, but is at the same time separate from it. It lives even when our flesh dies. That's the part of our child that we are trying to reach.

Once we make a connection between this part of our child and ourselves, then we can begin to train our child to want to make the right decisions and follow God.

Chapter Nine

GOLDEN RULES

*I*f you have already had your child baptized, do not worry. You did not harm them. What matters most now is what you do next, not what you did in the past. The longer you wait to implement changes in the direction your family is going, the harder that job will become. Children do not like change. The older they get, the more deeply engrained in a particular lifestyle they will likely be. It's important that rules don't change unless it is for a better reason that they understand. Taking things away defeats this purpose, and that's what changing to a Christian lifestyle will seem like to an older child. It is not impossible though. I have seen families change direction successfully that had older children when the process began. If you trust the Lord and depend on Him, He will help you accomplish this mission.

Rules should stem from your love of God coupled with your love for others. Not from manmade lists of things that you can do to make yourself more presentable to God. It's important for you to know that Jesus did all of the required "list" stuff on the cross at Calvary so that you can focus on living a joyful, prosperous, ritual-free life while sharing the love of Christ with others. Certain rules are important and always apply, but if we keep just two, then none of the others will ever come into question. What are the two? Love God with all your heart (all of who you are) and love others as you love yourself. If you can get those two down, you won't need any others. Either you'll want to please God in every aspect of your life (because you love Him so), or you won't want to do anything that would cause any other person harm (steal, lie, cheat, kill, etc.) because you love *them* so.

Too many rules are going to wear your child out fast and they will eventually give up. I have seen it happen. When children are forced into legalism (living like Puritans), they often bail out of that crazy plane the first chance they get. If rules consume a child's existence, they will not have enough wherewithal to concentrate on the God aspect of life, nor will they want to — even though it's right there before them. They will begin to reason, "If God has all these rules that are too hard to keep, I don't want any part of it." It is, however, possible to have rules that will be beneficial to the nurturing of your child's heart without causing them to be resentful.

On the other hand, no rules, or rules that are not followed by parents, will have the same undesired effect. We have played a game a few times over the years with teens where there are no rules. We'll put them out on a field, give them a ball, set up a couple goals, and then tell them to start. They are generally confused and ask what to do. They want to know what the rules are. We tell them there are no rules — just play. Go score points.

"How?" they want to know.

"It doesn't matter; there are no rules."

"How do you win?"

"However you want." It doesn't make much sense and isn't much fun. They get discouraged fast and most of them want to do something else. We emphasize the point that in order to have fun, there has to be rules, and in order to make sense, there has to be directions.

A few years ago, we had a teen come through our group that lived in a home with no rules. He governed himself. It was not going all that well. He was heavily involved with drugs and all the other things you might expect. He was interested in what we were doing, but had trouble sticking it out. One of my friends and fellow teen leaders was hoping that he might have one brain cell left to catch the message of the Gospel of Christ and turn his life around. We did a lot for him, including bringing him to a Christian camp. He even spoke out one night about his desire to follow Christ at one of our teen club gatherings. Unfortunately, his heart had not been prepared for any of this as a child and he was not able to make the transition. Shortly afterward, his lack of rules caught up to him and he ended up being placed in a state psychiatric facility where it is possible he may never leave.

This is only one case in hundreds of thousands and perhaps even millions of kids that have been raised without the training that God designed for them to be raised by. It is true that there are only 186,600 youths in the United States juvenile justice system, and only 70,000 teens in American prisons at a time, but there are ten times that amount wandering around as prisoners of their own freedom.[5] I have testified of the numbers of teens that I have dealt with that are living a sinful lifestyle due to their lack of being raised in the training of the Lord. I should point out here that—on the other hand—I have met many teens who were raised in the training of the Lord that are not suffering the fate of a godless upbringing. Instead, they love life and are enjoying it to the fullest. They are honorable, respectful, and enjoyable to be around. Their desire is to share the hope they have gained with those who are missing it and be a blessing in the lives of others.

God has a whole handbook of valuable child-raising techniques that truly work, and one of the biggest crimes of our age is that they are being ignored rather than vigorously utilized. That being said, the majority of the rules you maintain in your home should reflect the rules you find in the Bible. After all, the men who designed the framework for the rules that govern the United States of America put to use these same rules. If it was good enough for the wisest group of men that has lived since the time of David and Solomon, it should certainly work for us. It will take some time, but if you stick with it, God's rules will be the rules your child will want to keep. "It is sad to have a foolish child; there is no joy in being the parent of a fool" (Proverbs 17:21). But, a child who wants to follow God's way of thinking and grows wise will bring you great joy.

With God's help, you can make this truth happen. Mixed up in all of this will be things you never considered. Things like Santa Clause, the Easter Bunny, Halloween, and Rock and Roll. Neither David nor Solomon ever had to deal with any of these things, but you will. None of these "problems" are probably the toughest thing you'll ever face, but will still demand attention. I am not anti Santa Claus as much as I am pro wisdom. The only argument I had against Santa was that if I told my child he was real, I would automatically be creating future issues. One, I would be lying to her, and she was definitely going to find out someday really soon; and two, if everything I told her about Santa was a lie, what was she going to think deep down about Jesus? After all, they both have the same characteristics. They know when you've been sleeping; they know when you're awake. They even know if you've been bad or good, and both want you to be good for goodness sake.

I'm not a rocket scientist, but it doesn't take much imagination to figure out what a six-year-old child is going to think after their older friends spill the beans on Santa and they start hearing different ones say that God isn't real either. It's hard enough to get a child to see the forest through the trees without having to re-establish what truth is and what is not in their already fragile and unstable minds. I made it a point never to lie to my child so that she could always be sure that I was telling her the truth no matter what, and no matter how painful. This became especially difficult the day her mommy died. My wife had been involved in a hospital mishap that left her brain-dead. It took a couple days to figure out exactly what was going to happen, so we spent those days in a hospital waiting room with church friends and family members.

On the last afternoon, I looked around and noticed my daughter was missing. I went out in the hall where someone told me he saw her go into the chapel room. I entered, and as I looked around, there were small pews and a table up front with a cloth over it, but no daughter. I walked up front and peered under the tablecloth. There she was. In the midst of all the confusion, she had found her own little private tent. I crawled under the tablecloth and sat down beside her. "What's the matter, honey?" I asked.

With tears in her eyes, she said, "Mommy's never coming home again, is she?"

I looked straight at her and calmly answered, "No, honey, she isn't."

She sat there for a moment, and then said with reluctance in her voice, "Okay."

With that, we hugged. She wiped her tears, crawled out from under the table, and went back to the waiting room with the others.

I reasoned that even though it was a tough answer, and even though she had just turned six years old, she could deal with the truth because she trusted me. With Santa Clause, I didn't flat out tell her that he wasn't real. What I taught her was that only God had these kinds of abilities and challenged her to put two and two together. I would sneak around at Christmas and load up presents under the tree the night before. We even set cookies out. But the next morning she would smile and wonder when I was able to sneak all that stuff in and tell me she knew that I was the one who took a bite out of the cookie. It was fun for us. We played it out so that she wouldn't feel like she was being robbed compared to other kids, but at the same time she always felt one up on them because she knew the truth. She was concerned that her friends believed that Santa was real, so I also had to strongly caution her that it was not our job to warn the others. That would be completely up to their own parents.

Chapter Ten

RULES WERE MADE TO BE...

*R*ules in a Christian home should make sense when compared to what your child learns in the Bible. It is fairly certain that some will cause your child embarrassment until they learn the true reason for them and become convinced they are right. That's why it's important to not go overboard with rules and pick and choose your battles wisely. Nothing will turn a child bitter and drive them away faster than rules they do not agree with. If you keep trying to explain it every time the question comes up and have good reasons to back up what you are saying, they will keep trying to understand it until they finally get it. There is no exact set of rules that will work in every situation. I am including some basic practical thoughts here that may help you set your family's standards.

I imagine the first thing your child will have to deal with is toys. The main rule here is that all toys should be respectable. For girls, dolls should always be dressed modestly and their doll world should be a family friendly, God-honoring environment. Dolls shouldn't be complaining and arguing with one another. They do, especially when friends come over and join in the doll role-playing fantasy game, so you will have to keep an eye out for that and correct it when it happens. For boys, action figures, transformers, etc. should not portray evil beings, nor should their toys always be going around killing one another. Soldiers might be an exception because that's what soldiers do, and law officers do catch and sometimes kill bad guys. You will have to decide how extreme you become on such issues as you monitor your child's behavioral development. Toy world inhabitants, though, should learn to live in harmony wherever possible just as inhabitants of the real world should. That only makes sense.

Once this basic toy foundation is established, you can branch out from there. You should develop a good feeling for what is going to be harmful to your child's mental wellbeing and what is not. The decisions you make, even minor ones—like what toys are appropriate—are all part of the process that shapes who they become. I was not thrilled when someone gave my daughter her first Bratz doll, but she was willing to discard the scanty clothing and dress her modestly, so I dealt with it.

One game that I did insist on every year was a next level children's learning computer. Kids love them and they learn math, English, science, and social studies, as well as computer skills while they play. However, even those should have a daily time limit of one hour.

Shortly after dolls and action figures, the time for video games will arise. This is a touchy subject—especially if you play them yourself—but there are some important facts you should consider. Video games waste a lot of valuable time and are extremely addictive. In fact, teens play some kind of video game on average twelve hours per week. Many health problems arise in video game players, and in extreme cases have actually died from results of blood clotting after several hours of nonstop playing. Without rules, any teen could become an extreme case. In order to keep the peace, at some point you will inevitably have to give in to some form of video game acceptance.

Probably adapting the phrase *in moderation* would be the best way to approach video game usage. It would also be good to hold out as long as you can. Although experts do not agree on whether or not video game playing is bad, most agree that too much time spent playing video games is not healthy. Problems ranging from deep vein thrombosis, or blood clots to severe dehydration can affect long-term players. Poor school performance can also result as video game playing often substitutes for doing homework and reading. Another problem, of course, is the aggression that develops in a child as a result of violent video games. The Pew Research Center reported in 2008 that more than 90% of games rated as appropriate for children 10 years or older contained violence, including games rated "E" for everyone. (Most researchers define violence as the ability of a player to intentionally harm others in a game.) A variety of different studies do show that there is definitely a link between violent video games and increased aggressive behavior in youth.[6]

So, good boundary rules should be set in order to keep this potential problem from erupting. For a young child, fifteen minutes a day is plenty. What I found was that after explaining the pitfalls of video games and limiting the playing time to fifteen minutes a day, my daughter would play a couple days in a row and then it might be months before she asked to again. Experts suggest that one hour a day should be the maximum for teenagers. Content would be the second boundary to consider. No video games containing violence should be tolerated in your home. Maybe the experts are wrong, but even if they are, having your child become addicted to violent video games cannot possibly aid you in your quest to raise a godly child.

Next, before you know it, your child is going to "need" a cell phone. I know this is going to make me sound old school here, but I cannot get used to seeing kids going around talking and texting rather than paying attention to what's going on around them in the real world. It probably sounds a little crazy, but I set a rule for five minutes on the telephone with a friend when my daughter was very young. I reasoned that you can say whatever needs to be said in that amount of time and not waste the best part of your day (after school) on the phone. There were times when she would spend five minutes each with a couple different friends, but over time, the telephone lost its charm and she could go weeks without talking to anybody on it. That was, of course, until it was time for a cell phone. When she got her first cell phone, I didn't even know about texting. Talk about facing an enemy that you never saw coming.

You may simply decide no cell phone and that's that. If you allow a cell phone, then there should be set limits agreed upon before the cell phone arrives. Whatever rule applies to your landline home phone should also apply to a cell phone. It might pay to share one for awhile first as a break-in, training period. You will definitely need to set limits on texting. Although an average of two or three texts a day may not sound like much, your child will adapt to that and learn to live it with it just fine. As they get older, it might turn into a few more, but at the same time you will find that they may go several days with none.

You will also find that many of their friends will have their phone privileges suspended for abuse or be out of minutes often. This can be a good teaching opportunity to explain the consequences of poor planning and overindulgence. It should be a goal to use their minutes wisely, monitor them, and have plenty left at the end of each month. I am sure you have heard of instances where parents received surprise phone bills for hundreds of dollars. Although a child may be responsible for the bill, it is certainly not the child's fault. With a proper understanding of the privilege to even have a cell phone of their own, a child can quickly learn to use it responsibly. There is absolutely no reason for it to spiral out of control.

We now live in the age of technology and information. It is not a good idea to deprive our children of that, but it is a great idea to train your children to master technology, rather than let them become a slave to it. During the early years, it will be a good idea to limit computer time. Start out with fifteen minutes a day. Each year, that time could be extended a little — say to fifteen minutes twice a day, a half hour twice a day, and an hour twice a day, by the time they are sixteen or so. By then they will likely need time for reports and essays, as well as time for personal projects. Learning to use a keyboard and different computer functions at a young age is a good idea. Educational computer programs will help in this endeavor. Even in Christian education, the use of DVDs for classroom-style training and labs will probably be necessary for you soon.

No time alone on the Internet should be a rule until you are certain that your child understands the potential for danger that dwells there. Even then, usage should be limited to whatever sites you personally type in and pre monitor before you allow viewing. It is very possible to type in an address incorrectly and end up on a pornography site without warning. The next stage—which I would advise to start no younger than fifteen—would be to permit them to go to websites that you allow, but require permission each time they do. This will also help in the training process for what is acceptable and what is not. The Internet can be a huge asset for education and research. It can also be a cesspool for delinquency. It is imperative for children to learn early how to use it properly.

Even though you will have strict rules in place, you should still make an effort to block certain content from becoming available to your home. It has been determined that at least 66% of American households that contain children do not use parental controls or block websites deemed inappropriate for viewing.[7] There are many programs available that can filter Internet content according to the settings you deem appropriate. You should also password protect your computer and wifi access as well as not allow any devices that can obtain Internet access outside of your main family computer area. This should continue to be the "family" rule until you are convinced that it is your child's desire to avoid evil Internet content. This goal is well worth whatever the sacrifice or effort it takes to achieve. It will also be important to pray daily that God will give your child the strength to resist the temptations that will confront them through the various forms of technology available to them.

One of the pitfalls of the Internet is social networking. There are many negatives and few positives for children who become involved in this phenomenon. Unfortunately, the lure is there, and at some point you will probably have to give in to some form of it or another. A few walls need to be erected before social networking starts. Under no circumstances should anyone out there be able to discover the identity of your child through information they share on a social website. All information they send should only be accessible by people *you* know — not who they know. All "friend" requests should first be approved by you, and it's really important that they understand that social acquaintances on a website are not really friends at all. I'm not sure most kids today understand what the true meaning of a friend is.

They should learn to never give their name, school, street, town, or anything like that out on the Internet. There are predators lurking around every corner that prey on the innocent. You do not want to let your child make it easy for them. In fact, the more difficult it is, the more likely they are to be left alone. Nothing they do should become public information beyond the people that already know them. Everything should remain private within the circle that you monitor. None of this will make sense to a younger child, so it will be best to wait until they're at least fifteen before you give in to any type of networking. Plus, if you set an age requirement, it will give them something to look forward to, and by then you will have trained them in regard to what they should be watching out for.

Furthermore, chat rooms should be considered the devil's den. You need to instill this in their mind at an early age, because the temptation is constantly there. Don't even allow chatting with friends, because that will soon develop into chatting with others. A good rule is "we don't chat" period. Why? More than 30 percent of all people in chat rooms are not who they say they are. Your young daughter's new "friend" has a very good chance of being a sixty-year-old bearded man in sweat pants and no shirt with a bottle of whiskey in his hand. Eighty-nine percent of all sexual solicitations are made in either chat rooms or instant messages. One out of five kids have been solicited sexually online. One site has deleted over 90 thousand accounts in a two-year period because they were created by registered sex offenders, and I heard recently that the world's biggest social network is now going to allow known sex offenders to join its site.

If you do not have control over the lives of your children, you are likely not going to be able to stop this. If kids have access to chatting, they will chat. Over 15 million kids use instant messaging of some kind, and nine out of ten parents will never know if inappropriate contact has occurred. Over seven out of ten kids have been contacted by someone they do not know, and half of all children on the Internet have been asked to divulge personal information to total strangers. Fourteen percent of all children have actually met face to face with a stranger they were contacted by on the Internet. The solution is simple. You as the parent will have to take control of the situation until your children are old enough to understand the dangers and are willing to avoid them on their own.

For your child's own safety and wellbeing, they should also learn right away to never answer a cell phone call from any number they do not recognize. They should also never even open an email from anyone that they are not positive they know, let alone answer one. By following these simple rules and learning what kinds of clues a social network predator might be able to use in an effort to track them down, you can help them become a wise and worthy opponent for the world that will be trying to ruin them. A child with proper training will enjoy the challenge to avoid those who would wish to do them harm. They will understand completely the seriousness of the situation and actually recognize danger when they see it.

You will find that they will be bringing questionable situations to your attention and sharing with you what they see wrong about it.

Chapter Eleven

SUGAR PLUM FAIRIES
AND ROCK AND ROLL

*O*f course, interwoven into all of this is the need for your child to understand the true meaning of Christmas. For the most part, that probably goes without saying. Christmas, however, does break all the rules for saving money, spending wisely, and not spoiling a child. Focus on Christ can get lost quite easily in all of the Christmas hubbub. It just happens. So, at the heart of it all has got to be the story of Jesus. It's the only thing that keeps everything from swirling totally out of control. It will be your job to keep everything in perspective and maintain some kind of balance. Children for the most part want everything they see.

You will have to come to some kind of compromise, because even though it can be very bad to give a child everything they want, it can be equally as bad to give them nothing. Giving your child a lot is not the world's worst thing as long as they realize that everything they have comes from God and belongs to God. They need to understand that whatever they have has been given to them by God and they are expected to become wise caretakers of these possessions. At the same time, it is very important to live within your means. A wise child will come to understand their family's financial limitations and be appreciative of anything they might receive, understanding just as well as the one with many gifts that all blessings come from God.

The Easter Bunny raises quite a few concerns as well. The biggest one is that if you're not careful, it can easily take away the knowledge of why we celebrate Easter in the first place. In fact, more that 53 percent of kids today don't really know why. That's sad. Almost as sad, though, is what the Easter Bunny brings with him, and that's sugar. It is estimated that Americans eat 130 pounds of sugar a year. *I* estimate that kids eat the lion's share of sugar, so it's probably closer to 200 pounds a year for them and less for adults. We grew up thinking that sugar promoted tooth decay, and while I still believe that is true, it is now believed that sugar is actually toxic. Studies have shown it to cause obesity, type II diabetes, hypertension, heart disease, and cancer.

While it would be impossible to stop it all together, there are many ways to cut down on sugar intake. The first thing should be a no candy rule. I wasn't sure if this rule would work, but I met a twenty-one year old young man about ten years ago who told me his parents did not allow him to eat candy or drink soda when he was growing up. As I questioned him, I found that he never missed them, because he never had them and he had no desire for either as an adult. He stood about 6'4" and didn't have an ounce of fat on him. He is the only one I ever met who had this rule, so I have no one else to compare him to except my daughter, who is eighteen and has rarely ever had any candy or soda. She doesn't miss them either.

We do get a little sugar in foods like cereal (which is bad), but we have no white sugar in our home. We also skip dessert except for maybe once or twice a year, and the rest of the time abstain from cookies, cake, pies, and soda. During the summer, we usually have ice cream once a week, and in the winter hot chocolate once a week. Under these conditions we really don't miss it at all when we don't have it. We also don't have to have the medications necessary to calm kids down who intake excessive amounts of sugar. I'm not an expert at all, but when we take a busload of kids to a Christian camp it looks like a pharmacy in the area where they keep all the medications. These are the same kids I see eating a pound of candy a day and drinking a six pack of soda. Maybe there is no correlation, but then again, maybe there is.

Halloween is another tricky holiday that you are going to have to deal with. I personally look at it as satanic and try to avoid it all together. In order to help a child understand the lack of Halloween in their life, you may want to do fall or harvest decorating (no witches or goblins). Instead of trick or treating (which raises worse candy issues than Easter), we always spent the evening at a large store and bought a present like a doll or fish and arrived home after trick or treating time was over. In time, the question wasn't, "Why can't I go trick or treating like all my friends?" but "Where are we going shopping this year?" and "What can I get?" Problem solved.

The Tooth Fairy is the same kind of deal as Santa Clause. Right up front, the Tooth Fairy has got to be known as not real, but just a game you play. I always put some money under the pillow and then pretended it wasn't me, but my daughter always knew it was. I can tell you with certainty that it has caused no psycho-logical damage whatsoever for my child to know at a young age that false things are not real. I have, however, seen all kinds of psychological damage in kids that are taught that false things *are* real. I often wonder as I talk with these teens and try to convince them that God is real if deep down they feel like I'm trying to sell them a used Santa. Anyway, I find most of the time they're not buying. You know, "Fool me once, shame on you. Fool me twice, shame on me."

Many years ago, after making a decision to follow God, I had the leftover issue in my life of bad music. I was from the sixties and seventies music generation, so rock and roll was imbedded in my soul. The problem for me was I now got a seriously uneasy feeling as I listened to it. I knew that the people who were performing the music I was listening to were not following God, and if I sang along I was singing out against God's message. During that time, while attending a state fair, I came across a Christian radio station booth. The young man on duty talked with me a little about music, and it turned out that he had a similar love for rock and roll music when he first turned to God. He realized that his music was drawing his heart in the opposite direction of what he knew God would desire. The decision he made was to burn all of his music — CDs, cassettes, and records; all of it — and made a vow that he would only listen to God-honoring music.

I left there perplexed. I not only loved rock and roll music, I was also a collector. I had rare record albums from all over the world that even back then were worth ten times what they cost new. I was convicted though. The guy at the fair tent had given me a couple of sample Christian rock CDs. As I listened to them, I realized that it was the same instruments, but the music had a different message. I didn't feel it would be right to sell my collection to someone else, because instead of spreading the Gospel of Christ I would be poisoning the mind of whoever ended up with my albums. So I did the only logical thing I could think of—I disposed of them.

Today, eighteen years later, I am happy to report that for the most part, my family has been listening to God-honoring music since that time. Young people like different styles of music, some of which I cannot stand. Therefore, we have a few basic rules for music in our family. No matter how rocky or rappy it is, it has to be God-honoring, the people performing it have to be somewhat respectable-looking, and you have to be able to hear and understand the words. The only other thing to consider about music is headphone safety. Since volume settings vary, we decided that no more than halfway up would be plenty loud enough and probably would not do any harm to your hearing. There is overwhelming evidence that very loud headphone volume can cause permanent hearing damage, so it will be important to treat this as a health threat until your child fully understands the consequences.

Of course, there are a few times when you will have to bend the music rule a bit. Kid's songs like *I've Been Working on the Railroad* and *On Top Of Spaghetti* are technically breaking it, but you will have to use wisdom and budge a little here and there depending on the situation. You should have a line in the sand somewhere, though, that you will not cross. Ultimately, no matter what style of music your child prefers, if they love it and are hearing messages about God while they are listening to their favorite bands, it can only be a positive influence in their life. I hear Christian kids all the time saying how this song or that song has drawn them closer to God or inspired them spiritually. I've heard a lot worse from kids who have no music rules.

If you have a television in your home, then your job is just beginning. To do it right, it is going to cost a little.

Think of it, though, as an investment in your child's future. Over time, it will be money well spent. When they are young, you will be able to regulate pretty well what comes on the TV. Stay away from popular children's channels that display kids singing and playing secular music. If they don't know about them, they won't miss them. There are tons of Christian DVDs available for children that won't fill their minds with evil and Christian programs such as iShine that encourage children rather than teach them to act immorally.

As they get older, if you are going to watch any kind of television shows or movies, you should first buy a TV Guardian® language filter. This will take bad language out of any show on TV that has closed captioning. For movie DVDs, it would also be a good idea to invest in the Clearplay® system. This will filter bad language, violence, and immorality out of the movies you and your family watch in your home. Even though these devices (and monthly fee for Clearplay®) will tap into your budget a little, there is really no other option except to get rid of your TV and movies altogether. After awhile you will find that if the filtering isn't working on a particular show or movie, your child will actually tell you, "We can't watch this!" That'll be one of those "it's a proud day to be a parent" moments that almost all parents dream of.

Chapter Twelve

HOME AWAY FROM HOME

*A*ll the while this training is going on in your home, you should be mindful of the training possibilities that can be going on simultaneously outside of your home. If you choose wisely, outside forces can actually enhance everything you are trying to instill in your child's heart. I can confidently recommend a couple of organizations that will be of great assistance to you. One is the Awana® program. There are not too many areas that do not have a church somewhere around with an Awana program for kids, so I am fairly certain that you will be able to find one. You will love this benefit because their goal is to reach boys and girls with the Gospel of Christ. At preschool age, they start teaching children to learn Bible verses, interact, and play games together with other kids in a harmonious setting. It's a positive situation to help kids learn about Jesus and the Bible that doesn't have a downside.

Another equally good opportunity is Word of Life Clubs, and again, most areas have a church somewhere nearby that has a Word of Life Club. These clubs will teach your child to grow in Christ as well as how to get involved in Christian ministry. Word of Life club leaders in a local church have the support of a Word of Life local area missionary, as well as quality online teaching support.

Another great occasion to help your child grow spiritually and at the same time meet kids with similar backgrounds is a Christian summer camp. Probably the best known are summer camps sponsored by Word of Life out of Pottersville, New York. They go above and beyond to teach kids about Christ and the importance of following Him. They have weekly summer camping programs for all ages, including adults. If Word of Life is not available to you, I would suggest researching thoroughly before settling on just any Christian camp. Not all Christian camps are alike, and it will be very important to be sure what they teach before you send your children there. You don't want them ending up in a place that tries to undo everything you have been striving for.

While we're on the subject of social Bible clubs and Christian camps, it may be a good time to mention friendships. Obviously children need these and do develop them wherever they are. It would be important to help your children understand that in order to be a good friend, that person should be a believer in Christ and better yet, even more spiritual then they are. A strong spiritual friend will only help your child grow stronger spiritually, while a friend who is weaker spiritually can actually drag them down to a lower level. They should also learn that children who do not put any emphasis on a relationship with God should be considered as acquaintances or mission projects, but not someone to hang around with or consider a friend. As a teacher, if I advise you that it's okay to let your child be friends with the unsaved and it backfires, what does that make me? If I tell you that it is a bad idea because your child will surely learn more from a wayward friend than they will ever be able to teach them, in reality this can turn out to be very good advice. Sending your children to the wolves can be very risky business and rarely has any positive upside.

Another thing to consider seriously is whether or not to allow friendships with the opposite sex. Although most people do not agree with me, I would advise against it. In the long run, it may be a far better idea to keep girls with girls and boys with boys until the time for marriage comes. Involvement with members of the opposite sex can be a painful distraction that always has the looming potential for disaster. If you have that rule from the beginning, even though at a young age it doesn't make much sense, it will become clearer as your child grows older. On the other hand, if you allow it when they are young, it will make no sense when you try to change it as they grow older. It's always harder to play the game if the rules keep changing, especially when they get stricter.

Many years ago, a young girl attended our Sunday school a couple times a year when visiting relatives. She was active in many teen ministries in her area and competed in both regional and national Christian musical competitions. One year when visiting (now a teenager), she sat upstairs during the Sunday school hour sulking, and remained that way all through the main service as well. I found out later that the boy she had been dating had broken up with her. She was crushed and had been in this state for awhile. Why would a Christian family allow their child to be subjected to this kind of emotional torture when it is not necessary? There is no practical or Biblical reason to allow children to date before they are ready for marriage.

Just a couple years ago, an eleven-year-old boy brought his eleven-year-old girlfriend to our Bible club.

When someone mentioned it to me, I said, "Oh boy." I was scolded and told that they were just friends and it was "cute." The boy ended up moving away, so I don't know what is going on with him these days. I do know that the girl ended up pregnant at thirteen years old by another "friend." Whether boys and girls are just friends or if they are dating, it really doesn't matter. No matter what you call it, the potential for tragedy is always there. Whether or not it can be avoided will be determined by the choices you make as a parent. There are plenty of other more productive things they can be doing that will actually help them build for their future, rather than demolish it.

In most towns it is not uncommon to see children pushing their own children in strollers down the sidewalk. Many times the father is another child who is either no longer around or not even able to take care of himself, let alone a family. In these cases, both children have chosen the path that leads to ruin. Lives categorized by poverty and government assistance are normal outcomes in these situations. I try to instill in the minds of the teens I deal with that it is possible to break this pattern and enter life with a chance to succeed. Keeping their minds focused on God, education, and waiting until they are old enough to marry before having friends of the opposite sex will help greatly in this endeavor. Even though it is tough duty for a parent in the middle of it, by the time a child reaches marrying age, everyone will be happy.

I like comparing kids having friends of the opposite sex to raising a Bengal tiger cub. At first, little tigers are harmless, cute, and cuddly. As the tiger cub grows, it slowly becomes more dangerous and while no one's really paying attention it reaches the point where it now looks at your child as a potential next meal. There are many positive reasons to keep your child out of boy/ girl relationships until the time is right. Good advice here would be to teach your child to plan on dating the person they expect to marry after they have reached the age of twenty-one. Children, even at eighteen or nineteen years old have still not reached the age of who they will ultimately become. In other words, they are still in the process of changing and developing thoughts and systems of beliefs. How many people who were married young have ended up divorcing or being miserable because the person they're with now is not like the person they married?

In the Bible, when God brought the Israelites out of Egypt, they refused to enter the Promised Land because they did not trust God to protect them. The punishment they received was that none of the estimated two million people over twenty years of age would be allowed to enter the Promised Land...ever. Those twenty years old and below would still have the opportunity if they lived in a way that was God-honoring as they grew older. This could mean that those under twenty-one were still developing, while those twenty-one and over had primarily developed into who they would become. God considered them to be fully aware of why they were rebelling and responsible for their actions. I know there are exceptions to all rules, but for me, who I was when I was eighteen is not who I am now, but after twenty-one I had much of the same beliefs and traits that I still maintain today.

If your child decides to date an eighteen-year-old because they like what they see, it is not etched in stone that they will still see those same character traits in just a few short years. It's possible, but is it really worth the chance? It could turn out to be a huge, life-altering mistake for them. It seems far better to wait and find the one who remains consistent and does not change their way of thinking as they move into their early twenties. I have seen plenty of kids go through two years of Bible college, appearing to have a good handle on knowing God and living right, only to see them change their mind and follow after the world just a couple of years later. On the other hand, I do know many Bible-believing young adults who have been following the Lord from their youth and are now still following Him today. You can't know for sure what a person will become at any age I guess, but if they put their trust in God, He will help them find the one who has stayed on track. That's why I say that it would be far better to have them wait a little longer and actually get what they are bargaining for.

One way to help accomplish this is to have your child start preparing a list of ten or more desired qualities in a potential mate. At the top of the list should probably be that they have led a consistent Christian lifestyle growing up that has carried over into their early twenties. It will be surprising for them to see how some teen prospects that appeared to be solid Christians actually fall away when they leave home. You will be thankful that they did not date any of these before this happens. Plus, it will be much easier for you to help your child find the right mate that God has planned for them if they have not already fallen in love with the wrong one. God has made it clear that no one should choose a mate that does not put their faith and trust in Jesus Christ.

God refers to that as being unequally yoked. This can cause huge problems. The lesson in this is that a team of two pulling in opposite directions is not going to move forward without trouble, and will inevitably crash. Train your child early to understand this. If they hitch to the wagon of life with someone who is not on equal grounds spiritually, they will spend their life pulling a wagon that pulls back. There will be no unity concerning things like moral living, raising children, or worshipping God. A believer who marries an unbeliever will find that they have become a castaway on a lonely spiritual island.

Many teens these days are taking vows of sexual purity. This, of course, would be much easier to accomplish if they were not dating. Most parents do not have a no dating policy, which can only result from a serious lack of wisdom. Some teens that understand the importance of remaining pure have even decided to wait until their wedding day for their first romantic kiss. Those who have this plan will likely want to find a mate that has a similar desire. If God has instilled this goal in your child's heart, you can trust that He has already put someone out there who is searching for someone just like the child you are raising. It shouldn't be that hard for the two to find each other, especially with your assistance.

Chapter Thirteen

A FAMILY THAT PRAYS TOGETHER...

O ne of the things I've noticed about young teens who don't believe in God is that they have had absolutely nothing happen in their whole life that would lead them to believe there really is a God besides my say so. The only way I can think of to change that is to get God to do something that they see happen, knowing it can only be God doing it. The one surefire way to bring about a miracle like that is through prayer. Unfortunately, most parents don't pray with their kids much beyond the basics, and to get a kid to talk to God about things in their life on a regular basis by accident would be rare. So, they grow up only hearing about these things and never really witnessing them for themselves. It would be tough for anybody to believe in anything under those conditions.

On the other hand, if you start praying with your child on a regular basis about everything that's going on, sooner than later they are going to see miracles happening all over the place and they are going to know that God is doing them. As an example, we were praying the other night and mentioned an antique show that we were going to the next day. We prayed for safety and then asked God if we might find a treasure while we were there. It was an indoor show with over 200 dealers set up. When we walked in, I scanned the huge building and thought, *Somewhere out there is a hidden treasure.* Row after row we found nothing to speak of. With two rows left, I thought, *Well, Lord, if there's nothing in these two rows then I guess no treasure today.*

As I came down toward the end of the last row, I was looking at every single item in every booth. In the last booth I walked very slowly until I got to the end of it. I found nothing. I admit I was a little surprised, but I understood that it was up to the Lord and I was okay with that. My daughter had gone back to the restaurant area on the other side of the building to wait for me while I finished the last few rows. I headed back across the front, and about halfway down I looked over at a booth on the front wall and realized somehow I had missed it. I went in and around the horseshoe-shaped display area, and as I came to the end, I looked up to see a painting hanging there that was done in a style I recognized. At first I couldn't find the signature, but when I did, sure enough it was by an artist that I was familiar with. It was the last item in the last booth of the entire show.

I cannot explain the feeling that came over me. Even though I see God at work in my life every day, sometimes I get overwhelmed. All I could do was praise the Lord. You're probably wondering what it cost. I paid 20 dollars for it. It is worth more. I don't use the word "treasure" lightly. It's more important to stay focused on the point though. My daughter knows that I prayed about this because she was with me. She knows that God directed my steps that day and made sure that the very last thing I looked at in the entire building would

be that painting. She knows that there is no other expla-
nation for it and only God can do something like that.
This is not an isolated incident either. We pray together
for thirty to forty-five minutes every single night and
have since she was little.

I will say that she falls asleep most nights before we
are done praying. That part doesn't matter so much.
I fall asleep myself while I'm praying out loud some
nights. The important part is that we're praying together
and she sees God answering prayer on a regular basis.
There is no doubt in her mind, like there is no doubt in
my mind. If a shadow of doubt ever creeps in, I immediately think about some of the miraculous workings
of God I have witnessed in my life and the doubts flee
away. They can't stand against reality.

So, it is vitally important that you spend time in
prayer to God with your child. Ask for everything you
need according to His will and He will answer you. The
answers you receive are no more important than the
fact that your child is witnessing them being answered.
God uses these experiences to call your child to follow
Him. The child who isn't a part of a prayer life and
has never actually seen God answer prayer in a tan-
gible way might not hear God's call and end up like
the countless young people who do not believe in God.

Chapter Fourteen

PLAYING THE MONEY CARD

*I*t's only a guess, but probably nobody is going to get out of life without some kind of money problem at some point. So, it would seem like a good idea to train your child to handle money wisely and even more importantly, teach them how to handle problems. As part of that education, it would pay to have your child go through Dave Ramsey's Financial Peace University course. They may not be able to do everything recommended in this program, but certain things—like not abusing credit cards—are essential for them to learn. As hard as it may be to believe, more than a third of high school seniors have a credit card. By graduation, 80 percent of all college students will have at least one to four credit cards and maintain an average credit card debt of 4,100 dollars.[8]

Even though someone came up with the idea that a credit card would help a child become a good money manager, the truth is that all they do is teach kids to spend money they don't have until they reach the card limit. A debit card will do much the same as a credit card as far as accessing money or shopping online, without the risk of overspending or piling up credit card debt. I would add to that: you should also teach them to never risk money in any circumstance where there's a possibility it might be lost. It is far better to only gain a little in a secured investment than to loose money that is at risk. If you train your child to work hard, spend wisely, invest wisely, and trust in God, you will do well, and so will your child.

Another thing to consider is finding things that you can do at home with your child that will take their mind off the things of the world. Pay close attention to the gifts (talents) that God has given them. Help them develop those gifts with as much enthusiasm as you can muster. When my daughter was ten years old, she wanted to start sending a newsletter to her friends. We talked about possible names and she decided on The Christian Girls Club©. By age eleven she had the first one completed, which was only four pages long and went out to twelve people. The next one had a couple more pages and went out to a few more people.

Within a year, if I measured the cost, I would have had to say, "Forget it." It was somewhere around 65 dollars a month just for postage. Before long we had to buy a new color printer (no more black and white newsletters) and spend a couple hundred dollars on ink, paper, and envelopes each month. On top of that we had to spend hours printing, stapling, stuffing, and addressing envelopes. After a few years, it escalated into a full color magazine, and for Christmas 2012, The Christian Girls Club Magazine was a sixteen-page, full color magazine with 150 copies. That may not sound like a huge amount, but at age seventeen she did much of the writing as well as all of the set-up, design, editing, and publishing in her own home office. With God's help, no matter what your child's gift may be, you too can help them develop that talent into a useable talent for God's service.

Getting your child involved in some kind of family enterprise would not be a bad idea either. There are any number of things that you could "invent" as a family business in order to create a working relationship with your child. Anything from egg-laying chickens to going out and picking night crawlers would be a good idea. It should be something that you both have an interest in as well as make sense for the environment you live in. You won't want to try to raise sheep if you live in a condominium. They won't have to make a lot of money, and you will probably lose money if anything. But just working together with a parent in a harmonious relationship would be a dream come true for any child. It will also be a great opportunity to teach them real life lessons on the importance of honesty and integrity in the workplace.

Christian service is another great way to help your child grow closer to the Lord. Mission trips or volunteering a little time now and then with a Christian organization puts them in a position to both see God at work and meet other kids that have a heart to serve the Lord. Many times they build lifelong friendships and become actively involved in a network of solid Christian friends. The education that they will gain from any kind of ministry or family business will profit them with training and skills that they will be able to fall back on all through their adult lives. They will always remember what they learn from you, so the more positive instruction you can inject into their lives the better.Between what they learn from you and what they can learn from God's Word, they will have a firm foundation to build their life on. Of course, part of their future success may also require some college level courses. I personally would not recommend sending a child away to college unless they have a definite plan.

Obviously if they want to be a pastor, doctor, nurse, veterinarian, or anything that dictates years of schooling and training, they are going to have to attend college. For any abstract plans it would be best to follow up home school with some home college courses.

Before sending the ones off to school that have definite occupation plans that require a college degree, it would be a very good idea (if it were me, I would insist on it) to send them to the Word of Life Bible Institute for one year before you send them anywhere else. There they will receive the advanced Biblical training needed before venturing out into the world. It will be a follow-up to everything they have been learning from you at home over the years and will help prepare them for what they are going to face in a secular college. Even when the plan is to send them to seminary or some other Bible-based college, because Word of Life Bible Institute credits are transferable, there is everything to gain and nothing to lose.

Chapter Fifteen

THE RIGHT WAY IS NOT ALWAYS THE POPULAR WAY

*T*he suggestions I have included for you in this book may require a little tweaking in order to fit your family's lifestyle. It is important to note that at the heart of each suggestion there is a proven method for raising a God-honoring child, as well as a biblical principle. Not many people follow these guidelines, but then there are not a lot of God-honoring children either. Don't get me wrong. I am sure there are other methods that are equally as effective. I have had many people tell me I'm doing a good job one day and then criticize my methods the next. It goes with the territory, I guess.

The people in Jerusalem praised Jesus and shouted, "Hosanna in the highest!" as He entered the city on Palm Sunday. Five days later they shouted, "Crucify Him!" They didn't like His biblical methods either, and He's the Author of both the Bible and salvation. The important thing is to trust God for everything, and realize that if your methods are working, then they have to be from Him. You and I are not clever enough to come up with something on our own that will actually work for their salvation. God alone is the One who does the saving of

123

the child. It is neat that we as parents can have a part in it, actually playing out the role of "fishers of men." As the Apostle Paul said, "We are not saying that we can do this work ourselves. It is God who makes us able to do all that we do. He made us able..." (1 Corinthians 3:5-6)

Remember, you don't want to raise a robot. God doesn't want your child to be a puppy on a leash any more than He wants you to be a dog on a leash. Everybody has got to come to God of their own free will...not by being dragged to Him. That would not be acceptable to God any more than if He kept you on a leash because He knew if He let you loose you would run from Him. Your child has to learn from you the benefits of following Christ and putting Him first in their life. They should learn to do things because it is what God wants them to do. What God wants them to do and what they want to do should be the same thing. They should learn to live lives that are pleasing to God not because they have to, but because they want to. It has to become who they are — not what we want them to be.

It may be that you have wished for awhile now that you could get a chance to start your life over. You're been going in the wrong direction and there has to be more to life then what you've seen so far. The need to lead your baby to God is the chance you have been waiting for. Take it, because chances to start over and reasons to take those chances rarely come. Now is the time to act. If you take it step by step you will succeed and ultimately find a life worth living.

Rather than getting your baby baptized, commit yourself as a parent to raise your baby in the teaching of the Lord and to lead this child by godly principles into adulthood and, ultimately, their own personal walk with God.

FOR FURTHER STUDY

I encourage you to read my book *Which God Should I Choose?* and share it with your friends and family. In fact, quite a few people have informed me that they enjoyed reading it out loud together with other family members as part of their family devotion time.

One of my favorite authors and speakers is Dr. John Barnett. He is a very interesting and knowledgeable teacher that you can trust. If you Google his name or go to dtbm.org you can find out more about him.

Ray Prichard is another personal favorite that you will also like. You can find out about him at keepbelieving.org, and also listen to sermons, watch videos, or buy his books there.

Other truthful authors and speakers that you can trust are Dr. Erwin Lutzer, Woodrow Kroll, Adrian Rogers, Mike Calhoun and Ken Ham. There are, of course, many others, but these would be a good place to start and then branch out from their recommendations. As I mentioned, you must be very careful when choosing Bible teachers, because unfortunately, there are many false ones.

I would also recommend going to wol.org and checking out their summer speaker schedule. Most of these guest speakers are also authors and can be trusted to share God's Word accurately.

Also, while on their webpage, you may want to check out the summer camping schedule. Word of Life, in Schroon Lake, New York, has week-long Bible conferences throughout the summer with campsites available at the Word of Life Family Campground, or deluxe rooms at the Word of Life Inn. The Bible teachers that speak at these week long retreats are among the finest in the world.

Finally, I encourage you to visit the Creation Museum in Petersburg, Kentucky. They do far more than counter the evolutionist's phony claims; they prove that they cannot possibly be true. You can also learn more about creation at answersingenesis.org.

IN CLOSING

*I*f this book has helped you in some way to grow closer to the Lord, then I encourage you to send an email and let me know. My email address is save-done95@gmail.com.

The Bible says, "Let the redeemed of the LORD say so, Whom He has redeemed from the hand of the enemy" (Psalm 107:2 [NKJV]) and, "If you declare with your mouth, 'Jesus is Lord,' and if you believe in your heart that God raised Jesus from the dead, you will be saved." (Romans 10:9).

We would like to help you do that (declare that Jesus is your Lord) by placing your name "on the cross" at our website as one who has put their faith and trust in Jesus for their salvation. Our website address is which-godshouldichoose.com. This will be your chance to proclaim across the World Wide Web that you are a follower of Jesus Christ.

Endnotes

1. Tertullian *On Baptism*, ch. 18 (*ANF* 3:677-78)
2. http://www.monitoringthefuture.org/data/11data.html
3. http://www.troubledteen101.com/articles36.html
4. www.nydailynews.com/.../1-12-teens-attempted-suicide-report-article...
5. http://yellodyno.com/Statistics/statistics_mental_health.html
6. http://www.foxnews.com/health/2012/08/13/teens-and-video-games-how-much-is-too-much/
7. Internet content control
8. http://www.credit.com/press/statistics/student-credit-and-debt-statistics.html

*B*en Kniskern's book Which God Should I Choose? is designed for many situations. It answers the questions of those seeking true spiritual guidance by examining facts concerning the cults and religions of today. It also provides proven direction for finding the key that unlocks the door to true inner peace and happiness for their lives. Because of the extensive research and easy-to-understand summary of the facts contained on its pages, Which God Should I Choose? can also be considered as a useful tool to assist those who share their faith with others. Finally, Which God Should I Choose? offers a perfect gift opportunity for graduates, family members, and friends that you have been praying will find their way to the right God.

CPSIA information can be obtained at www.ICGtesting.com
Printed in the USA
BVOW072008220413

318820BV00001B/2/P